CORYDON

ANDRE GIDE
CORYDON

TRANSLATED AND INTRODUCED
BY RICHARD HOWARD

Original French edition first published 1925 by Editions Gallimard.
This English translation published 1985 as a Gay Modern Classic
by GMP Publishers Ltd, P O Box 247, London N15 6RW.
Original French edition copyright 1925 Editions Gallimard.
Translation copyright © 1983 Farrar, Straus and Giroux, Inc.

British Library Cataloguing in Publication Data

Gide, André
    Corydon. – (Gay Modern Classics)
    1. Homosexuality
    I. Title II. Series
    306.7'66   HQ76.25

    ISBN 0-907040-54-3
    ISBN 0-907040-53-5 Pbk

Cover: *Melampus and the Centaur* by Glyn Philpot (1884-1937).
Reproduced by kind permission of Glasgow Museums and Art Galleries

Printed and bound by Billing & Sons Ltd, Worcester

Contents

Translator's Note

In 1951, the year of Gide's death (and a year to which, in a moment, I shall have occasion to recur with regard to Gide's life and my own peremptory appearance in it), I remember reading a book called, irresistibly, *The Homosexual in America: A Subjective Approach*, though nothing of what I read has remained with me so tenaciously over these three decades as the contumely in Auden's voice—it must have been one of the first times those chortling accents had been sounded in my vicinity —conceding that the author of such platitudes might serve valiantly enough as one's congressman, say, but was hardly apt to do justice to the complexities so desperately engaged . . . What also remains is the author's *name*, for it was Donald Cory, and even in those unguarded pre-*Lolita* days when we were not in the habit of weighing the evidence of authorship so fastidiously as "Harold D. Doublename, a misty-eyed left-wing professor at a Midwestern university" would require us to do, it had occurred to me that someone (a Mr. Edward Segarin, it turns out) had chosen to advance thus tricked out under the reversed and naturalized *nom de plume* (in this case, a white feather indeed) of Gide's momentous myth, translated for the first time into English only the year before without a translator's name attached. If "Donald Cory" sought protection, even a kind of pedigree, under the minatory wing of "Corydon," might I not loiter a little over that disputed or deferred identity: who is Corydon, that he should be thus commended, and by so many others abused, ever since?

Well, certainly he was a shepherd in Virgil's second Eclogue, in the first line of which we learn that he burned for fair Alexis (another shepherd). To the classically educated Frenchman, the name alone would be, even now, an indication of sexual status, though in *our* pastoral tradition—in Spenser, for example—Corydon is but a shepherd quite as susceptible of being matched with a shepherdess.

Gide was fond of these names which strew the Theocritan canon—such titles as *Mopsus* and *Amyntas* are to be found in his work before and after *Corydon*; but more important still to my question, or to an answer to it, is the character Menalchas (Ménalque), who first appears in 1895 in a prose fragment of that name, later incorporated into *Les Nourritures terrestres* (1897), poetical apostrophes to hedonist liberation (even from hedonist liberation), an attack on conformity of all kinds. Apparently *The Immoralist*, which Gide published in 1902, was to have been a life of Ménalque before it became Michel's interior drama; the rather "nineties" tempter and catalyst, evidently drawn from

Translator's Note

Gide's observations of Oscar Wilde, is yet endowed with a resonance we recognize in another connection:

Lately an absurd, a shameful lawsuit with scandalous repercussions had given the newspapers a convenient occasion to besmirch his name; those whom his scorn and superiority offended seized this opportunity for their revenge; and what irritated them most was that he seemed quite unaffected. "You have to let other people be right," was his answer to their insults. "It consoles them for not being anything else." But Society was outraged, and those who, as the saying goes, "respect themselves" felt obliged to cut him, thereby requiting his contempt. . . .

Obviously this is the same man who, "I had been told, made no objection to certain unnatural tendencies attributed to him." Gide has managed to assimilate much of what remains outside his fictions in the figure of Ménalque, and not only the "I" of *Corydon*—a frequently boorish, utterly un-Gidean bigot—but Corydon himself are the book's real success (as we so often feel that Plato's real success is the figure of Socrates and the decor of the polis, the attribution to philosophy of a site and a voice). Some of the best comic touches occur at the very beginning of Gide's little subversion:

On entering his apartment, I admit I received none of the unfortunate impressions I had feared. Nor did Corydon afford any such impression by the way he dressed, which was quite conventional, even a touch austere perhaps. I glanced around the room in vain for signs of that effeminacy which experts manage to discover in everything connected with inverts and by which they claim they are never deceived. However I did notice, over his mahogany desk, a huge photographic reproduction of Michelangelo's "Creation of Man," showing Adam naked on the primeval slime, reaching up to the divine Hand and turning toward God a dazzled look of gratitude. Corydon's vaunted love of art would have accounted for any surprise I might have shown at the choice of this particular subject. On the desk, the portrait of an old man with a long white beard whom I immediately recognized as the American poet Walt Whitman. . . .

It is only when we have savored the "huge photographic reproduction . . . showing Adam naked on the primeval slime" and the portrait of an old man with a long white beard, immediately recognizable to the nameless speaker, that we will be prepared for the wicked parody of this scene that Nabokov gives us in *Lolita* (chapter 2, section 6); Humbert Humbert is delighted to discover some comfort in the analogous sufferer and pederast Gaston Godin, who "always wore black, even his tie was black; he seldom bathed. . . . Upstairs he had a studio —he painted a little, the old fraud. He had decorated its sloping wall (it was really not more than a garret) with large photographs of pensive André Gide, Tchaikovsky, Norman Douglas, two other well-known English writers, Nijinsky (all thighs and fig leaves), and Marcel Proust. All these poor people seemed about to fall on you from their inclined plane." By the time Gide got to *Corydon*, the century had turned and the pervert's lair was no longer the incense-blued den of decadence (pages of illustrations)—yet we recognize in Corydon's asceticisms, just as surely, the necessary props and signs. Only our narrator is taken in.

To be taken in—to be deceived, especially self-deceived—was Gide's abomination. It was what he knew to be wrong with his culture, and especially with his comfort. And it was the one realm—the realm of lies and fraudulence—where he could be roused from his own lair, even by a college student. In 1951, I began to say a moment ago, Robert Gottlieb and I, as editors of the *Columbia Review*, wrote a letter to André Gide: would he like to speak, in his trenchant magisterial way (we didn't actually say that, but we let it be suspected), to our situation from his; would the man who had written "I believe that what is called 'experience' is often but an unavowed fatigue, resignation, blighted hope" care to address himself to a group of attentive students who had in common, chiefly and precisely, their inexperience? And, of course, their fervor for his achievement, which so paradoxically seemed to be the encoding of his . . . experience? Gide answered, not trenchantly or magisterially, but with a seemly generosity, just one month before he died; his letter, translated by our professor and his old friend Justin O'Brien, sounds the voice of the prepared (the overprepared?) Counselor of Youth, a letter useful on almost any occasion, rather what we hear—the resonance of the frowning public man—in the replies of the old Goethe or the old Hugo to like solicitations, for in the history of literary effrontery there are always "like solicitations":

Translator's Note

That I am touched by the homage of certain young people
of your university, expressed by your most courteous
letter, goes without saying. But I should like to be sure
there is no misunderstanding, and that their attention is
indeed such as my writings deserve. It is essential not to
make a mistake about this. I never laid claim to providing
the world with a new doctrine. And indeed I have often
deserved the reproach of not stating quite clearly what I
wanted and of not defining in detail rules of conduct which
might have given hope of saying what we feel to be in
danger today: a culture slowly and painfully acquired
throughout centuries, which belongs to a common heritage
and seems to have ceased to be of value today. New values
have replaced those which formerly allowed us to commune
together, which provided us with a reason for living and
for sacrificing ourselves for them. I believe that if we let
ourselves be stripped of that past, we shall experience a
forever irreparable loss, all the more tragic since the new
generations will not even be aware of their impoverishment.

But to tell the truth, surrounded by blasted hopes, I am
getting to the point of no longer really knowing to what to
apply my ardor and my allegiance. On the other hand, I
know ever more clearly what I do not want, what I cannot
accept, and against what my whole being revolts: falsehood. Whether it comes from the right or from the left,
whether it be political or religious, falsehood tends to
suppress human personality by depriving it of the right to
free inquiry. It is the stifling of the individual with the
hope of an illusory advantage to the herd. Each of us is
asked to abdicate his critical spirit in order to make it

easier to strangle himself. This is what we must not accept. How readily I subscribe to Jean-Jacques Rousseau's admirable statement: "He who prefers truth to fame may hope to prefer it to life."

I have no doubt of being in complete agreement, on this point, with you, young representatives of a country which has done more than any other to teach and to protect that "self-reliance" of which your Emerson speaks so eloquently and without which we are at the mercy of those who would exploit us. Refusal to tolerate falsehood, either in others or in oneself, is the watchword around which I think we can and must rally.

With every sympathy and, despite everything, hopefully, your most attentive

André Gide

I do not think the letter needs—or indeed can sustain— much analysis; it was certainly the making of our "Gide issue," as I am convinced the old man knew it would be, for he wrote it out by hand, and it is characteristically *ondoyant* in its evasion of real platitudes, as of real plunges into the depths. As the years have gone by, plunges seem less and less appropriate, and the steadfast refusal to lie (Gide leaves out the "social" as a likely source of untruth, perhaps because he had so much exposed "society" in his own fictions, as in these dia- logues) glows quite steadily enough to constitute a declarative beacon played on a much-vexed darkness— not the darkness I needed to plunge into, back in 1951, of course, but an outer darkness, the kind that usually gains so ruinously upon the inner one. Enough that

Translator's Note

Gide's letter—and for this I give it here—constituted a first contact with the master, if not the mastery, of what the London *Times* in its obituary of Gide, the next month, termed his "heterodoxy" (homosexuality?). Or if not mastery, then acknowledged mystery—at least, acknowledgment.

The pursuit of truth, and its essential Gidean corollary, the refusal to lie, make *Corydon* worth retranslating. For despite his painstaking recourse to an appallingly rigged and anthropomorphized zoology, despite his other recourse—the two are always found together in the period's apologies for *the homosexual in society*— to the literary and historical vestiges of Greek culture, Gide was on to something; indeed, the very indecisiveness of his vocabulary affords us a clue which his first translator chose to overlook. Precisely when we are discovering that there is no such massive and unitary object of discourse (or experience) as *homosexuality*, Gide's fluctuations in nomenclature must be rendered as an index of a mind reluctant to dignify confusion by calling it uniformity. The terms may seem to us merely quaint—"uranism," "pederasty," "inversion," "degeneracy," not to mention "Urnings" and "The Third Sex" —but at least they question, they even jeopardize conventions of classification which, as Michel Foucault observes, impose upon us a false unity of conceptualization. Like the Freud he had not read, and the Lawrence who never read him, Gide suggests, in the very variety of his nomenclature as well as in his liberalizing proposals to a relentlessly repressive and therefore libertine society, that the language of desire is not "about" a continuous, unitary sexual experience. Rather that language produces and constitutes that experience. What we say structures "instinct"—it generates the scripts in which experience and sensation in themselves are registered and understood. This insight warrants, it seems to me, a good many pages of cockchafers and costumed Hellenizing.

Begun in 1907, *Corydon* endured if it did not sustain a gestation of thirteen years; published—as "C.R.D.N." and consisting of but the first two dialogues and a bit of the third—in an unsigned private edition of twelve copies in 1911, and in 1920 in a similarly unsigned private edition of twenty-one copies consisting of all four dialogues and a preface, and in 1925 it was to be published in a signed, commercial edition, much reprinted subsequently. In 1921, determined upon its general publication (a determination in part effected by the wrenching alienation from his wife, who had burned all his letters to her upon the realization that Gide had accompanied young Marc Allégret to England), Gide made a great discovery. He began to read Freud, the Freud who seemed to echo his own thoughts when, in 1905, he had written:

psychoanalysis resists entirely the attempt to regard homosexuals as a specially formed group and to separate them from other men. . . . It finds that all men are capable of a homosexual object choice and that they have in fact performed it unconsciously. . . . The exclusive sexual interest of a man for a woman is equally in need of explanation and cannot be taken for granted as an underlying chemical attraction.

Translator's Note

So delighted, and so excited, was Gide to learn that Freud regarded a man who experienced *no* homosexual desires rather than one who did as the true "deviant," statistically speaking, that he asked Mrs. Bussy to consider whether her brother, James Strachey, Freud's English translator, might not intercede for him: would not Freud be the indicated, the ideal *authority* to supply a preface to *Corydon*, thereby sheltering it from so many of the misconceptions and antagonisms it was bound to provoke? Apparently communications broke down somewhere between Dorothy Bussy, James Strachey, and Vienna, but it is worth noting that Gide actually began psychoanalytic treatment (five sessions) at about this time, and that he went so far as to speculate, "Perhaps I might present *Corydon* as 'translated from the German' . . . a preface by Freud might emphasize the book's usefulness and timeliness" (April 1921). What matters is that we realize that the perceived congruity of purpose between Freud and Gide echoes a larger historical structure: the apprehension of unity within apparently opposed or agonic energies, whether sexual or psychic. *Corydon* is one of the books we must read to understand the development of the Western mind in the first quarter of the twentieth century.

In this perspective, *Corydon* takes its place in the intuition of ecstatic wholeness which to me appears to be the ruling metaphysical pathos of its period. From *The Immoralist* and *Les Nourritures terrestres* (contemporaries of late Nietzsche and early Freud) to *Corydon* and *If It Die* . . . (contemporaries of early Mann and late Proust), Gide undertakes an apprehension of dis-

cursively determined rhapsodic experience unequaled
for the scope and frankness of its scrutiny. Gide's secret,
as Camus remarked, is that he never lost, among all his
doubts, the pride of being human (*i.e.*, more interested
in harmony than in doctrine). His is not a great mind,
Forster said in *his* obituary, but a free one—"and free
minds are as rare as great, and even more valuable at
the present moment." To call *Corydon* dated is to remark its affinities with other formal responsibilities of
its date: it demands—and deserves, in its effort to dis-
cern not the nature of human sexuality but the history of
its repression—our closest attention as it peers, grace-
fully, at times grotesquely, "beneath the veil of lies, convention and hypocrisy which still stifles an important and
not contemptible part of humanity."

Richard Howard
1983

Preface to the Third Edition

My friends insist that this little book is of the kind which
will do me the greatest harm. I do not believe it can rob
me of anything I value; or rather: I do not believe I
value greatly what it will rob me of: applause, decora-
tions, honors, entrée into fashionable circles are not
things I have ever sought out. I value only the esteem of
several rare minds who will understand, I hope, that I
have never deserved it more than by writing this book
and by daring to publish it today. I hope not to forfeit
such esteem, yet I should certainly rather lose it than
owe it to a lie, or to some misunderstanding.

I have never sought to please the public; but I value
to excess the opinion of certain individuals; this is a
matter of sentiment, and nothing avails against it. What
has sometimes been taken for a certain intellectual timidity was in most cases nothing but the fear of grieving
such people; of grieving one soul, in particular, who
has always been dear to me above all others. Who can
say how many hesitations, reticences, and evasions are
the consequence of sympathy, of affection? —With regard to mere postponements, I cannot regard them as

Preface to the Third Edition

regrettable, convinced as I am that artists today would often have benefited from a certain ripening. Ideas which at first attract and seem to dazzle us fade by the next day or soon thereafter. That is why I have waited so long to write this book and, having written it, to publish it. I wanted to be sure that what I was propounding in *Corydon*, and what seemed to me obvious, I would not soon have to retract. But no: my ideas have merely been confirmed in the meanwhile, and what I now have against my book is its reserve, its timidity. In the more than ten years since it was written, new examples, arguments, and evidence have corroborated my theories. What I believed before the war I believe more strongly today. The indignation *Corydon* may provoke will not keep me from believing that what I say here must be said. Not that I believe one should say all that one thinks, and say it no matter when—but precisely what I am saying here must be said, and must be said today.*

* Certain books—Proust's in particular—have accustomed the public to be less alarmed by, and to consider more deliberately—what it previously pretended or preferred to ignore. For how many of us suppose they can suppress what they ignore! . . . But such books have greatly contributed, I fear, to our current confusion. The theory of the ⌐woman-man, of the *Sexuelle Zwischenstufen* (intermediate degrees of sexuality) advanced by Dr. Hirschfeld in Germany quite some time before the war—and which Marcel Proust appears to accept—may well be true enough; but that theory explains and concerns only certain cases of homosexuality, precisely those with which this book does not deal—cases of inversion, of effeminacy, of sodomy. And I realize today that one of my book's great shortcomings is in fact its failure to deal with them, for they turn out to be much more frequent than I previously supposed.

Even granting that Hirschfeld's theory accounts for these cases, his "third sex" argument certainly cannot explain what we habitually call "Greek love": pederasty—in which effeminacy is neither here nor there.

Preface to the Third Edition

Certain friends to whom I had first shown this book criticized me for an excessive concern with questions of natural history—not that I am actually mistaken in attributing so much importance to them, but—they said —such questions will tire and deter the reader. —Indeed, that is just what I hope for: I am not writing to entertain, and I intend to disappoint from the start those seeking pleasure, art, wit, or anything but what will ultimately be the simplest expression of a very serious theme.

Finally, I certainly do not believe it is true wisdom to abandon oneself to nature and to give the instincts free rein; but I do believe that before seeking to subdue and tame them, we must understand them fully—for many of the discords we now endure are no more than apparent and due solely to errors of interpretation.

November 1922

Preface to the Second Edition

After waiting eight years, I have decided to reprint this little book. It was published in 1911, in an edition of twelve copies which were put away in a drawer—from which they have not yet emerged.

That first *Corydon* included only the first two dialogues and the first part of the third. The remainder of the book was merely sketched. Friends dissuaded me from completing it. "Our friends," Ibsen says, "are dangerous not so much for what they make us do as for what they keep us from doing." Yet the considerations I was setting forth in this little book seemed to me of the greatest importance, and I believed it necessary to present them. But on the other hand I was a firm believer in public decorum and quite prepared to conceal my views if I thought they might jeopardize law and order. This was the reason, rather than any personal precautions, which relegated *Corydon* to a drawer and kept it there so long. Nonetheless, during recent months I have become convinced that this little book, however subversive it might seem, attacked only falsehood after all, and that nothing is actually unhealthier, for an individual and for a society, than an accredited lie.

After all, I thought, what I have to say about such things does not bring them into existence. They *exist*. I am trying to explain what exists. And since in most cases no one is willing to admit that *such things exist*, I am examining, I am trying to examine, whether it is really as deplorable as it is said to be—that such things exist.

1920

FIRST DIALOGUE

In the year 190_, a scandalous trial raised once again the irritating question of uranism. For eight days, in the salons as in the cafés, nothing else was mentioned. Impatient with theories and exclamations offered on all sides by the ignorant, the bigoted, and the stupid, I wanted to know my own mind; realizing that reason rather than just temperament was alone qualified to condemn or condone, I decided to go and discuss the subject with Corydon. He, I had been told, made no objection to certain unnatural tendencies attributed to him; my conscience would not be clear until I had learned what he had to say in their behalf.

It was ten years since I had last seen Corydon. At that time he was a high-spirited boy, as gentle as he was proud, generous and obliging, whose very glance compelled respect. He had been a brilliant medical student, and his early work gained him much professional approval. After leaving the lycée where we had been students together, we remained fairly close friends for a long time. Then several years of travel separated us, and when I returned to Paris to live, the deplorable reputation his behavior was acquiring kept me from seeking him out.

On entering his apartment, I admit I received none of the unfortunate impressions I had feared. Nor did Corydon afford any such impression by the way he dressed, which was quite conventional, even a touch austere perhaps. I glanced around the room in vain for signs of that effeminacy which experts manage to discover in everything connected with inverts and by which they claim they are never deceived. However I did notice, over his mahogany desk, a huge photographic reproduction of Michelangelo's "Creation of Man," showing Adam naked on the primeval slime, reaching up to the divine Hand and turning toward God a dazzled look of gratitude. Corydon's vaunted love of art would have accounted for any surprise I might have shown at the choice of this particular subject. On the desk, the portrait of an old man with a long white beard whom I immediately recognized as the American poet Walt Whitman, since it appears as the frontispiece of Léon Bazalgette's recent translation of his works. Bazalgette had also just published a voluminous biography of the poet which I had recently come across and which now served as a pretext for opening the conversation.

i

"After reading Bazalgette's book," I began, "I don't see much reason for this portrait to be on display here."

First Dialogue

My remark was impertinent; Corydon pretended not to understand. I insisted.

"First of all," he answered, "Whitman's work remains just as admirable as it ever was, regardless of the interpretation each reader chooses to give his behavior . . ."

"Still, you have to admit that your admiration has diminished somewhat, now that Bazalgette has proved that Whitman didn't behave as you so eagerly assumed he did."

"Your friend Bazalgette has proved nothing whatever; his entire argument depends on a syllogism that can just as easily be reversed. Homosexuality, he postulates, is an unnatural tendency . . . Now, Whitman was in perfect health; you might say he was the best representative literature has ever provided of the natural man . . ."

"*Therefore* Whitman wasn't a pederast. I don't see how you can get around that."

"But the work is there, and no matter how often Bazalgette translates the word 'love' as 'affection' or 'friendship,' and the word 'sweet' as 'pure,' whenever Whitman addresses his 'comrade,' the fact remains that all the fervent, tender, sensual, impassioned poems in the book are of the same order—that order you call *contra naturam*."

"I don't call it an order at all . . . But how would you reverse his syllogism?"

"Like this: Whitman can be taken as the typical normal man. Yet Whitman was a pederast . . ."

"*Therefore* pederasty is normal . . . Bravo! Now all you have to prove is that Whitman was a pederast. As far as begging the question goes, I prefer Bazalgette's syllogism to yours—it doesn't go so much against common sense."

"It's not common sense but the truth we should avoid going against. I'm writing an article about Whitman—an answer to Bazalgette's argument."*

"These questions of behavior are of great interest to you?"

"I should say so. In fact, I'm writing a long study of the subject."

"Aren't the works of Moll and Krafft-Ebing and Raffalovich enough for you?"

---

* Bazalgette is certainly entitled to his choice (indeed the French language obliges him to choose) whenever the *gender* of the English word remains uncertain, and to translate, for instance, *the friend whose embracing awakes me* by "l'amie qui," etc.—though by doing so he is deceiving both the reader and himself. But he is not entitled to draw conclusions from a text after he himself has corrupted it. He admits with disarming candor that the affair with a woman which he describes in his biography is "purely" imaginary. His desire to locate his hero in heterosexuality is such that when he translates "the heaving sea" as "la mer qui se soulève" he feels obliged to add "comme un sein"—"like a breast," which in literary terms is absurd and profoundly uncharacteristic of Whitman. Reading such words in his translation, I rush to the original with the *certainty* there has been a . . . mistake. Similarly when we read "mêlé à celles qui pèlent les pommes, je réclame un baiser pour chaque fruit rouge que je trouve," it goes without saying that the feminine gender is Bazalgette's invention. There are any number of such examples—and *there are no other kind,* by which I mean the kind which might allow Bazalgette to proceed as he has; so that it is really to his translator that Whitman seems to be speaking when he exclaims *I am not what you suppose!* As for the purely literary distortions, they are sufficiently frequent and significant to denature Whitman's poetry in a strange way. I know few translations which betray their author more completely . . . but this would take us too far . . . from our subject, I mean.

"Not enough to satisfy me. I'd like to deal with the subject in a different way."

"I've always thought it was best to speak of such things as little as possible—often they exist at all only because some blunderer runs on about them. Aside from the fact that they are anything but elegant in expression, there will always be some imbecile to model himself on just what one was claiming to condemn."

"I'm not claiming to condemn anything."

"I've heard that you call yourself tolerant."

"You don't understand what I'm saying. I see I'll have to tell you the title of what I'm writing."

"By all means."

"What I'm writing is a *Defense of Pederasty*."

"Why not a *Eulogy*, while you're at it?"

"A title like that would distort my ideas; even with a word like 'Defense,' I'm afraid some readers will take it as a kind of provocation."

"And you'll actually publish such a thing?"

"Actually," he answered more seriously, "I won't."

"You know, you're all alike," I continued, after a moment's silence; "you swagger around in private and among yourselves, but out in the open and in front of the public your courage evaporates. In your heart of hearts you know perfectly well that the censure heaped on you is entirely deserved; you protest so eloquently in whispers, but when it comes to speaking up, you give in."

"It's true that the cause lacks martyrs."

"Let's not use such high-sounding words."

"I'm using the words that are needed. We've had Wilde and Krupp and Eulenburg and Macdonald . . ."

"And they're not enough for you?"

"Oh, victims! As many victims as you like—but not martyrs. They all denied—they always will deny."

"Well of course, facing public opinion, the newspapers or the courts, each one is ashamed and retracts."

"Or commits suicide, unfortunately! Yes, you're right, it's a surrender to public opinion to establish one's innocence by disavowing one's life. Strange! we have the courage of our opinions, but never of our behavior. We're quite willing to suffer, but not to be disgraced."

"Aren't you just like the rest, in avoiding publication of your book?"

He hesitated a moment, and then: "Maybe I won't avoid it."

"All the same, once you were dragged into court by a Queensberry or a Harden, you can anticipate what your attitude would be."

"I'm afraid I can. I would probably lose courage and deny everything, just like my predecessors. We're never so alone in life that the mud thrown at us fails to dirty someone we care for. A scandal would upset my mother terribly, and I'd never forgive myself. My younger sister lives with her and isn't married yet—it might not be so easy to find someone who would accept me as his brother-in-law."

"Well, I certainly see what you mean; so you admit that such behavior dishonors even the man who merely tolerates it."

"That's not an admission, it's an observation of the facts. Which is why I'm looking for martyrs to the cause."

"What do you mean by such a word?"

"Someone who would forestall any attack—who without bragging or showing off would bear the disapproval, the insults; or better still, who would be of such acknowledged merit—such integrity and uprightness—that disapproval would hesitate from the start . . ."

"You'll never find such a man."

"Let me hope he'll appear."

"Listen, just between ourselves: do you really think it would do much good? How much of a change in public opinion can you expect? I grant that you're a little . . . constrained. If you were a little more so, it would be all the better for you, believe me. Such wretched behavior would come to a stop quite naturally, just by not having to put itself on show." I noticed that he shrugged his shoulders, which didn't keep me from insisting: "Don't you suppose there are enough turpitudes on display as it is?" And I permitted myself to remark that homosexuals find any number of *facilities* in one place or another. "Let them be content with the ones that are concealed, and with the complicity of their kind; don't try to win the approval or even the indulgence of respectable people on their behalf."

"But it's the esteem of just such people I cannot do without."

"If you can't do without it, then change your behavior."

"I can't do that. It can't be 'changed'—that's the dilemma for which Krupp and Macdonald and the rest saw no other solution than a bullet."

"Luckily you're less tragic."

"I wouldn't swear to it. But I would like to finish my book."

"Admit that there's more than a little pride in your case."

"None whatever."

"You cultivate your strangeness, and then in order not to be ashamed of it you congratulate yourself on not feeling like all the rest."

He shrugged again and walked up and down the room without a word; then, having apparently overcome the impatience my last remarks aroused:

ii

"Not so long ago, you used to be my friend," he said, sitting down again beside me. "I remember that we could understand each other. Is it really necessary for you to make such a show of sarcasm each time I say a word? Of course I'm not asking for your approval, but can't you even listen to me in good faith—the same good faith in which I'm talking to you . . . at least, the way I *would* talk if I felt you were listening . . ."

"Forgive me," I said, disarmed by the tone of his words. "It's true that I've lost touch with you. Yes, we were once quite close, in the days when your behavior still held out against your inclinations."

"And then you stopped seeing me; to be frank about it, you broke off relations."

"Let's not argue about that; but suppose we talked the way we used to," I went on, holding out my hand. "I have time to listen to anything you have to say. When we used to see each other, you were still a student. Did you already have such a clear notion of yourself back then? Tell me—I want to know the truth."

He turned toward me with a new expression of confidence, and began:

"During my years as an intern in the hospital, the awareness I came to of my . . . anomaly plunged me into a state of mortal distress. It's absurd to maintain, as some people still do, that you only come to pederasty because you're seduced into it, that it's the result of nothing but being dissipated or blasé. And I couldn't see myself as either degenerate or sick. Hard-working and extremely chaste, I was living with the firm intention, once my internship was over, of marrying a girl who has since then died, and whom I used to love above anything else in the world.

"I loved her too much to realize clearly that I didn't desire her at all. I know that some people are reluctant to admit that the one can exist without the other; I was entirely unaware of it myself. Yet no other woman ever haunted my dreams, or wakened any desire in me whatever. Still less was I tempted by the prostitutes I saw almost all my friends chasing. But since at the time I hardly suspected I might actually desire others altogether, I convinced myself that my abstinence was a virtue, gloried in the notion of remaining a virgin until marriage, and prided myself on a purity I could not suppose was a delusion. Only gradually did I manage to understand what I was; finally I had to admit that these notorious allurements which I prided myself on resisting actually had no attraction for me whatever.

"What I had regarded as virtue was in fact nothing but indifference. This was an appalling humiliation—how could it be anything else?—to a rather high-minded young spirit. Only work managed to overcome the melancholy which darkened and diminished my life; I soon persuaded myself I was unsuited for marriage and, being able to acknowledge none of the reasons for my depression to my fiancée, my behavior toward her became increasingly evasive and embarrassed. Yet the few experiments I then attempted in a brothel certainly proved to me that I wasn't impotent; but at the same time they afforded convincing proof . . ."

"Proof of what?"

"My case semed to me altogether exceptional (for how could I suspect at the time that it was common?). I saw that I was capable of pleasure; I supposed myself incapable, strictly speaking, of desire. Both my parents were healthy, I myself was robust and energetic; my appearance revealed nothing of my wretchedness; none of my friends suspected what was wrong; nothing could have persuaded me to speak a word to a soul. Yet the farce of good humor and risqué allusions which I felt obliged to act out in order to avoid all suspicion became intolerable. As soon as I was alone I slipped into despondency."

The seriousness and the conviction in his voice compelled my interest. "You were letting your imagination run away with you!" I said gently. "The fact is, you were in love, and therefore full of doubts. As soon as you were married, love would have developed quite naturally into desire."

"I know that's what people say . . . How right I was to be skeptical!"

"You don't seem to have hypochondriacal tendencies now. How did you cure yourself of this disease of yours?"

"At the time, I did a great deal of reading. And one day I came across a sentence which gave me some sound advice. It was from the Abbé Galiani: 'The important thing,' he wrote to Mme d'Epinay, 'the important thing is not to be cured but to be able to live with one's disease.' "

"Why don't you tell that to your patients?"

"I do, to the incurable ones. No doubt those words seem all too simple to you, but I drew my whole philosophy from them. It only remained for me to realize that I was not a freak, a unique case, in order to recover my self-confidence and escape my self-hatred."

"You've told me how you came to realize your lack of interest in women, but not how you discovered your tendency . . ."

"It's quite a painful story, and I don't like telling it. But you seem to be listening to me carefully—maybe my account will help you speak of these matters less frivolously."

I assured him, if not of my sympathy, at least of my respectful attention.

"You already know," he began, "that I was engaged; I loved the girl who was to become my wife tenderly but with an almost mystical emotion, and of course with my lack of experience I scarcely imagined that there could be any other real way of loving. My fiancée had a brother, a few years younger than she, whom I often saw and who felt the deepest friendship for me."

"Aha!" I exclaimed involuntarily.

Corydon glanced at me severely. "No: nothing improper took place between us; his sister was my fiancée."

"Excuse me."

"But you can imagine my confusion, my consternation when, one evening of heart-to-heart exchanges, I had to acknowledge that this boy wanted not only my friendship but was soliciting my caresses as well."

"Your tenderness, you mean. Like many children, after all! It's our responsibility, as their elders, to respect such needs."

"I did respect them, I promise you that. But Alexis was no longer a child; he was a charming and perceptive adolescent. The avowals he made to me then were all the more upsetting because in every revelation he made, all described with precocious exactitude, I seemed to be hearing my own confession. Nothing, however, could possibly justify the severity of my reaction."

"Severity?"

First Dialogue

"Yes: I was scared out of my wits. I spoke severely, almost harshly, and what was worse, I spoke with extreme contempt for what I called effeminacy, which was only the natural expression of his feelings."

"It's hard to know how to deal with such cases."

"I dealt with this one so badly that the poor child—yes, he was still a child—took my scolding quite tragically. For three days he tried with all the sweetness in his power to overcome what he took to be my anger; and meanwhile I kept exaggerating my coldness no matter what he said, until it happened . . ."

"What happened?"

"Then you didn't know that Alexis B. committed suicide?"

"But you wouldn't go so far as to suggest that . . ."

"No, I'm not suggesting anything at all. At first it was said to be an accident. We were in the country at the time: the body was found at the foot of a cliff . . . An accident? I suppose I could make myself believe anything. But here's the letter I found next to my bed."

He opened a drawer, took out a sheet of paper with a shaking hand, glanced at it, and then said:

"No, I'm not going to read you this letter; you would misjudge the child. The substance of it—and written in the most moving way—was the agony our last conversation had caused him . . . especially certain remarks I had made. 'To spare yourself this physical torment,' I had shouted in a fit of hypocritical rage against the inclinations he was confessing to me, 'the best thing you could do would be to fall in love.' *Unfortunately*, he wrote me, *I have fallen in love, but with you, my friend.*

First Dialogue

You haven't understood me and you feel contempt for me; I see that I am becoming an object of disgust to you—as I am for myself for that very reason. If I can't change my awful nature, at least I can get rid of it ... Four more pages of that slightly pompous pathos characteristic of that stage of life, the kind of thing it becomes so easy for us to call declamation."

This story had made me more than a little uncomfortable ... "Of course," I said at last, "such a declaration, and made to you specifically, was a nasty trick of fate; I can understand that the episode must have affected you."

"To the point that I immediately gave up all thoughts of marrying my friend's sister."

"But," I went on with my train of thought, "I'm more or less convinced that each of us gets the disasters he deserves. You must admit that if this boy hadn't sensed in you some possible response to his own guilty passion, that passion ..."

"Maybe some obscure instinct could have made him aware of it, as you say; but in that case, what a crying shame that same instinct couldn't make me aware of it too."

"What if you had been aware—what would you have done?"

"I think I could have cured that child."

"You were just saying that these were incurable cases; didn't you just quote the Abbé's words—'the important thing is not to be cured ...' "

"All right, enough of that! I could have cured him the same way I've cured myself."

16

"And that is . . ."

"By convincing him he wasn't sick."

"Why don't you just come right out and say that the perversion of his instinct was natural!"

"By convincing him that the deviation of his instinct was quite natural."

"And if you had it all to do over again, you would have yielded to him, *naturally*."

"Oh, that's another question altogether. When the physiological problem is solved, the moral problem begins. No doubt my feelings for his sister would have led me to try to argue him out of this passion, in the same way that I would no doubt have tried to argue myself out of my own; but at least this passion itself would have lost that monstrous character it had assumed in his eyes. —This drama, by opening my own eyes to my own nature, showing me the real nature of my feelings for this child, this drama I've thought about so long has finally determined my attitude toward . . . the particular thing you find so despicable; in memory of this victim, I want to cure other victims suffering from the same misunderstanding: to cure them in the way I just told you."

iii

"I think you understand now why I want to write this book. The only serious books I know on this subject are certain medical works which reek of the clinic from the very first pages."

"So you don't plan on writing as a doctor?"

"As a doctor, a naturalist, a moralist, a sociologist, a historian . . ."

"I didn't know you were so protean."

"I mean I'm making no claims to speak about my subject as a specialist—only as a man. The doctors who usually write about the subject treat only uranists who are ashamed of themselves—pathetic inverts, sick men. They're the only ones who consult doctors. As a doctor myself, those are the ones who come to me for treatment too; but as a man, I come across others, who are neither pathetic nor sickly—those are the ones I want to deal with."

"Yes, with the normal pederasts!"

"Precisely. You understand that in homosexuality, just as in heterosexuality, there are all shades and degrees, from Platonic love to lust, from self-denial to sadism, from radiant health to sullen sickliness, from simple expansiveness to all the refinements of vice. Inversion is only one expression. Besides, between exclusive homosexuality and exclusive heterosexuality there is every intermediate shading. But most people simply draw the line between normal love and a love alleged to be *contra naturam*—and for convenience's sake, all the happiness, all the noble or tragic passions, all the beauty of action and thought are put on one side, and to the other are relegated all the filthy dregs of love . . ."

"Don't get carried away. Sapphism actually enjoys a certain favor among us nowadays."

He was so worked up that he completely ignored my remark and continued his argument.

First Dialogue

"Nothing could be more grotesque than the spectacle, whenever there's a morals case in the courts, of the righteous indignation of the newspapers at the 'virile' attitude of the accused. No doubt the public expected to see them in skirts. Look: I cut this out of the *Journal* during the Harden trial . . ."

He searched among various papers and handed me a sheet on which the following was underlined:

Graf von Hohenau, tall in his tight-fitting frock coat, dignified and even stately, gives no impression of being an effeminate man. He is the perfect type of the Guards officer, entirely committed to his profession. And yet this man of martial and noble bearing is charged with the gravest offense. Graf von Lynar, a man of prepossessing appearance as well . . . etc.

"In the same way," he went on, "Macdonald and Eulenburg seemed, even to the most prejudiced observers, intelligent, handsome, dignified . . ."

"In short, desirable from every point of view."

He said nothing for a moment, and I saw a look of scorn flash across his face; but recovering himself, he continued as if he had not caught my meaning.

"One is justified in expecting the object of desire to have some beauty, but not necessarily the subject of it. I am not concerned with the beauty of these men. If I made a point, just now, of their physical appearance, it is because it matters to me that they be healthy and virile. And I am not claiming that every uranist is any such thing; homosexuality, just like heterosexuality, has its degenerates, its vicious and sick practitioners; as a doctor, I have come across as many painful, distressing, or dubious cases as the rest of my colleagues. I shall spare my readers that experience; as I've already said, my book will deal with healthy uranism or, as you just put it yourself, with *normal pederasty*."

"Didn't you understand I was using the phrase derisively? It would be all too easy for you if I conceded this first point."

"I shall never ask you to concede anything just to please me. I prefer you to be obliged to do so."

"Now it's your turn to be joking."

"Not in the least. I'm willing to bet that in twenty years it will be impossible to take words like 'unnatural' and 'perverted' seriously. The only thing in the world I concede as not natural is a work of art. Everything else, like it or not, belongs to the natural order, and once we no longer consider it as a moralist, we had better do so as a naturalist."

"The words you indict have their uses—at least they reinforce our decency. Where would we be, once you had suppressed them?"

"We wouldn't be any more demoralized than we are; and I'm making a conscious effort not to add: 'On the contrary!' . . . What frauds you heterosexuals are—to hear some of you tell it, it's enough for sexual relations to be between different sexes to be permissible; at least, to be 'normal.' "

"It's enough for them to be so potentially. Homosexuals are depraved by nature—necessarily."

"Do you really suppose that self-denial, self-control, and chastity are entirely unknown to them?"

"No doubt it's a good thing that laws and human respect occasionally have some hold over them."

"Whereas you think it's a 'good thing' that laws and conventions have so little hold over *you*?"

"I'm coming to the end of my patience with you! Look, on our side we have marriage, honest marriage, which I don't imagine is to be found on yours. You make me feel like one of those moralists who regard all extramarital pleasures of the flesh as sin and who condemn all relationships that are not legally sanctioned."

"Oh, I'm more than a match for them there, and if you were to encourage me, I could turn out to be even more intransigent than they are. Of all the conjugal beds I've been called upon to examine as a physician, I assure you that very few were made with clean linen, and I wouldn't like to wager that more ingenuity, more perversity, if you prefer, is always to be found among prostitutes than in certain 'honest' households."

"You're disgusting."

"But if the bed is a conjugal one, then whatever vice is there is immediately laundered."

"Surely married couples can do whatever they like; that's their privilege. And besides, it's none of your business."

" 'Privilege'—yes, I like that word much better than 'normal.' "

"I had been warned that the moral sense was strangely warped among your kind. But I'm amazed to discover to what a degree. You seem to have completely lost sight of this natural act of procreation—an act which marriage sanctifies and which perpetuates the great mystery of life."

"And once performed, the act of love is at liberty to run wild—no more than a gratuitous fantasy, a game. No, I'm not losing sight of that; in fact, it's on that finality that I want to construct my own ethics. Apart from procreation, nothing remains but the persuasions of pleasure. But think it over for a minute—the act of procreation need not be frequent: once every ten months is sufficient."

"That's rather seldom."

"Very seldom; especially since nature suggests an infinitely greater expenditure; and . . . I hardly dare finish my sentence."

"Go on—you've already said so much."

"All right, then: I maintain that far from being the only 'natural' one, the act of procreation, in nature, for all its disconcerting profusion, is usually nothing but a fluke."

"You'd better explain that one!"

"I'll be glad to, but it brings us to natural history; that's where my book begins and how I approach my subject. If you have a little patience, I'll tell you what I mean to say. Come back tomorrow. By then I'll have put my papers into something like order."

SECOND DIALOGUE

The following day, at about the same time, I returned to Corydon's apartment.

"I nearly decided not to come back," I told him as I came in.

"I knew you would say that," he answered, as he invited me to sit down—"and that you would come all the same."

"That was clever of you. But if you don't mind, it's not the psychologist I've come to listen to today—it's the naturalist."

"And it's as a naturalist that I'm prepared to speak to you, set your mind at rest. I've arranged my notes—not all of them: three volumes wouldn't be enough for that, but as I told you yesterday, I am deliberately putting aside the medical observations; not that they don't interest me, but they make no immediate claim on me —my book has no need of them."

"You speak as though it were already written."

"It's all worked out, at least; but there's more than enough material . . . My subject falls into three parts."

"So that natural history will take up the first part?"

"Enough to last us for today."

"May I ask what will be included in the second part?"

"If you come back tomorrow, we'll talk about history, literature, and the arts."

"And the day after tomorrow?"

"I'll do my best to satisfy you as a sociologist and a moralist."

"And after that?"

"After that I'll say goodbye and let others have their say."

"Meanwhile, you're the one I want to listen to. Why don't you begin."

i

"I admit to taking a few rhetorical precautions. Before approaching the question, I'll quote from Pascal and Montaigne."

"What do they have to do with such matters?"

"Listen. Here are two sentences I want to use as my epigraph; it seems to me they set the argument on the right footing."

"Let's hear them."

"This one you probably know—it's from Pascal: *I am very much afraid that this nature is itself merely a first form of custom, just as custom is a second nature.*"

"I think I may have seen that . . ."

"I'm going to underline '*I am very much afraid*' . . ."

"Why?"

"Because I'm glad he's afraid. It's with good reason."

"And let's hear the Montaigne."

Second Dialogue

"The laws of conscience, which we say are born of nature, are born of custom."

"I know you're well-read. Anyone can find what he wants in a well-stocked library—if he looks long enough. What difference does it make if you pick a random line from Pascal and interpret it as you please—you can't really think you'll get much support from Pascal that way!"

"Don't you suppose there were plenty of citations to choose from? I've copied out any number of sentences that show I'm not distorting Pascal's intentions. Read these . . ."

He handed me a sheet of paper on which the following words were transcribed: *Man's nature is entirely natural,* omne animal. *There is nothing that is rendered natural, as there is nothing natural that may be lost.*

"Or, if you prefer . . ."

He handed me another sheet, on which I read: *Doubtless nature is not entirely uniform. It is custom which therefore makes it so, for it constrains nature; and sometimes nature surmounts custom and confines man within his instinct, despite every custom, good or bad.*

"Are you claiming that heterosexuality is simply a matter of custom?"

"No, only that we judge by custom when we claim that heterosexuality alone is natural."

"Pascal would be flattered if he knew what turns you were making him serve!"

"I don't think I'm distorting his ideas. What's important is to realize that where you say 'against nature' the phrase 'against custom' would do. Once we are convinced of that, I hope we can approach the subject with less prejudice."

"Your quotation is a double-edged sword, and I can turn it against you: the customs of pederasty, imported from Asia or Africa into Europe, and from Germany, England, or Italy into France—such customs may have contaminated us here and there, now and then. God be thanked, the natural instincts of good old France have always turned up again, robust and lively as one might expect, even ribald if need be . . ."*

Corydon stood up and paced the room a few moments in silence. Finally he continued.

"I must beg you, my dear friend, not to bring nationalism into the argument. Wherever I have traveled in Africa, the Europeans are convinced that this vice is licit; opportunities abounding and the beauty of the people encouraging them, they give freer rein to their impulses than in their own country; as a consequence the Moslems are convinced that these tastes have been brought to them from Europe . . ."

"You wouldn't argue, though, that example and encouragement have their part to play—and the laws of imitation . . ."

"Don't you realize that they function just as powerfully in the other direction? Remember La Rochefoucauld's profound remark: *There are people who would never have loved if they hadn't heard others speak of love.* —Just think how in our society, in our behavior,

* "If there is one vice or one sickness repugnant to French mentality, to French morality, to French health, it is—to call things by their name—pederasty" (Ernest Charles, *Grande Revue*, July 25, 1910).

28

everything predestines one sex to the other; everything teaches heterosexuality, everything urges it upon us, everything provokes us to it: theater, literature, newspapers, the paraded example set by our elders, the ritual of our drawing rooms and our street corners. *Given all that, failing to fall in love is a sign of ill breeding!* crows Dumas *fils* in his preface to *La Question d'argent.* Yet if a young man finally succumbs to so much collusion in the world around him, you refuse to grant that his decision was influenced, his desire manipulated if he ends up making his choice in the 'right' direction! And if, in spite of advice, invitations, provocations of all kinds, he should manifest a homosexual tendency, you immediately blame his reading or some other influence (and you argue in the same way for an entire nation, an entire people); it has to be an acquired taste, you insist; he must have been taught it; you refuse to admit that he might have invented it all by himself."

"I refuse to admit that he might have invented it if he's healthy, precisely because I do not acknowledge this taste as a spontaneous one except among those who are inverted, degenerate, or sick."

"What, then! Here is this taste, this tendency which everything conceals and everything thwarts, which is forbidden to show itself in either art, or books, or life, which the law condemns as soon as it declares itself and which you pillory with shame and mockery, exposing it to insult and injury and almost universal contempt . . ."

"Keep calm, keep calm! Your uranist is a great inventor."

"I'm not saying he always invents—I'm saying that

when he imitates it's because he wants to imitate; I'm saying that the example corresponded to his secret preference."

"You do insist that this preference is innate . . ."

"I am simply stating a fact . . . And you will permit me to remark that this taste, moreover, can scarcely be inherited, for the plausible reason that the very act which would transmit it is necessarily a heterosexual act . . ."

"An ingenious conceit."

"You have to admit that this appetite must be very powerful, deeply ingrained in the flesh, actually irrepressible, or to use the word again, quite 'natural' in order to withstand these vituperations and utterly refuse to disappear. Don't you think the appropriate comparison is to a persistent spring which is assiduously dammed up here and which gushes out there, since it's impossible to quench the source itself. Condemn it all you like! Repress it, oppress it—you'll never suppress it!"

"I grant you that in recent years the cases reported by the press have become deplorably frequent."

"That's because a few famous trials have given the papers the opportunity and the habit of speaking freely about it. Homosexuality seems more or less frequent according to whether it appears more or less openly. The truth is that this instinct which you call against nature has always existed to about the same extent in all places and all times—like all the natural appetites."

"Tell me Pascal's phrase again: *All tendencies are in nature . . .*"

Second Dialogue

"Doubtless nature is not entirely uniform. It is custom which therefore makes it so, for it constrains nature; and sometimes nature surmounts custom and confines man within his instinct . . ."

"I'm beginning to understand you better. But by that reckoning, you'll have to classify sadism and murder and even the rarest and worst instincts as natural too . . . So where will you be then?"

"I do believe, in fact, that there is no instinct that can't be warranted by some animal custom. Cats never enjoy their lovemaking without mixing a few bites with their caresses. But here we're digressing; especially since I believe, for reasons easy enough to fathom, that sadism more readily accompanies heterosexuality than uranism . . . Let's say, for simplicity's sake, if you like, that there are social instincts and antisocial instincts. Whether pederasty is an antisocial instinct is a subject I examine in the second and third parts of my book. Let me postpone the question for now. First I must not only establish and acknowledge homosexuality as natural, but also try to give a reasonable explanation for its existence. Perhaps these preliminary remarks were not out of place, since I might as well tell you—what I am about to formulate is nothing less than a new theory of love."

"I suppose the old one wasn't good enough for you?"

"Apparently not, since it tends to make pederasty into an enterprise *contra naturam* . . . We live buried up to our eyes—and our brains—in a very old and very common theory of love it no longer occurs to us to argue about; this theory has penetrated very deeply into natural history, distorting much of our reasoning and perverting much of our observation; I am afraid it will be difficult to release you from it in a few minutes of conversation . . ."

"You can always try."

"Especially since everything I'm about to say to you depends on my doing so."

ii

He walked over to the bookshelves and leaned against them.

"A great deal has been written about love; but love's theorists are rare. Actually, since Plato and the guests at his *Symposium*, I recognize none except Schopenhauer."

"M. de Gourmont has recently written on the subject . . ."

"It amazes me that so subtle a mind should have failed to unmask this last refuge of mysticism; that his relentless skepticism did not recoil from the implied metaphysical finality of a theory which makes love into the dream of all nature and the mating instinct into the secret spring of life. In fact, it amazes me that this often ingenious mind could not reach the conclusions I'm about to put to you. His book *The Physiology of Love* is inspired by a single concern: to reduce human love to the level of animal mating—a concern I shall call zoomorphic, the worthy counterpart of the anthropomorphism which discovers human tastes and passions in everything . . ."

Second Dialogue

"Suppose you get on with your new theory."

"I'll give it to you straight off, in its initially monstrous and paradoxical form. Later we can touch it up a little here and there. Here it is then: love is an entirely human invention—it does not exist in a state of nature."

"Then you agree with de Gourmont that what we call 'love' is nothing but the sexual instinct more or less well disguised. That may or may not be true, but it is certainly nothing new."

"No, no! I'm saying that these antitheists who claim to replace God with some enormous idol they call the 'universal instinct of reproduction' are merely self-deceived, in a strange way. What M. de Gourmont is offering us is an *alphysics of love*, whereas I claim that this famous 'sexual instinct' which irresistibly drives one sex toward the other is of their own invention, and that such an instinct does not exist."

"Don't try to intimidate me by your peremptory tone. What can this denial of the sexual instinct mean when the whole theory of instincts, in its most general form, is being questioned and challenged by Loeb, Bohn, etc.?"

"I wasn't presuming that you were familiar with the detailed work of those gentlemen."

"I admit I haven't read them all."

"Or that I was addressing a scholar rather than an old friend in whom I detect a certain ignorance with regard to natural history . . . Oh, don't protest: you share such ignorance with more than one literary man.

Second Dialogue

Neither qualified to argue the subtler points of the question nor to define in so many words the invariably vague limits of a notion like 'instinct,' and knowing that some people enjoy attributing to the words 'sexual instinct' a specific and categorically imperative force functioning like other instincts with the precision of an infallible mechanism,* and to which, according to M. de Gourmont, 'obedience is ineluctable,' I say to you with assurance: no, that instinct does not exist."

"I see that you're playing with words. *In reality*, your Bohn prudently remarks in a recently published book, *the danger lies not in using the word 'instinct' but in not knowing what can be behind this word, and in employing it as an explanation.*† I grant him that. You're still admitting the sexual instinct, and I hardly see how you could do otherwise; only you're denying that this instinct has the automatic precision some people attribute to it."

---

* ". . . If the nervous system is centralized, as in the case of weevils, their enemy the cerceris gives only one stab; if movements depend on three ganglia, then three stabs are inflicted; if there are nine ganglia, then nine stabs; the bristly ammophila does the same when it needs the grubs of the so-called gray-worm moth for its own grubs; if a thrust into the cervical ganglion seems too dangerous, then the predator contents itself with slowly chewing in order to induce the necessary degree of immobility," etc. (for instance, Remy de Gourmont, *loc. cit.;* according to the observations of J. H. Fabre. See the excellent critique of this mythology by Marchal, reported by Bohn, *Nouvelle psychologie animale*).

Almost all this dialogue was written in the summer of 1908. Bohn's *Nouvelle psychologie animale* had not yet been published, and I had not yet come across Max Weiler's memorandum *Sur la modification des instincts sociaux,* 1907, whose theories virtually coincide with what I am arguing here.

† Bohn, *loc. cit.*

"And claiming that it naturally loses more and more precision as we rise in the animal scale."

"So that you'd say it is never more indeterminate than in man."

"We'll not be discussing man today."

"Whether precise or not, this instinct is transmitted; it has played a role and proved itself adequate in that role."

"Yes: adequate . . . just that."

He stopped, rested his forehead on his hand, and seemed for a few minutes to be collecting his thoughts; then, looking up, he continued.

"You use these words, 'sexual instinct,' to cover a bundle of automatisms or at least of tendencies which are solidly linked together in the lower species but which, as you ascend the steps of the animal ladder, become dissociated more and more easily and more and more frequently.

"In order to keep these tendencies linked together, certain concomitances are often required—certain connivances, certain complicities which I shall discuss later on—and without whose cooperation the bundle comes undone, letting the tendencies scatter. This instinct is not, so to speak, homogeneous; for the pleasure which the act of procreation affords either sex is not, as you know, necessarily and exclusively linked to this act.

"Whether, in the course of evolution, pleasure precedes or follows the tendency does not concern me for the moment. I grant that pleasure accompanies each act in which the vital activity is asserted, so that, in the sexual act, which simultaneously involves the greatest expenditure and the perpetuation of life, pleasure attains to orgasm . . . And no doubt this creator's labor, so costly for the individual, would not be achieved without such conspicuous recompense—but pleasure is not so closely linked to its goal that it cannot easily be separated and freed from it.* Henceforth pleasure is pursued for itself, without concern for fertilization. It is not fertilization the animal seeks but simply pleasure. The animal seeks pleasure—and finds fertilization by accident."

"No doubt it took nothing less than a uranist to discover such a splendid truth as that."

"Perhaps in fact it took, as you say, someone disturbed by the prevailing theory. Kindly notice that Schopenhauer and Plato realized that their theories would have to take uranism into account; they could not do otherwise; indeed, Plato assigned it so important a role that I can well understand your feeling alarmed by it; as for Schopenhauer, whose theory prevails, he regards uranism as a kind of exception to the rule, an exception which he explains plausibly but imprecisely, as I shall show you later on. In biology as in physics, I grant you that the *exceptions* alarm *me*; my mind stumbles over them, refractory to a natural law which applies only with reservations—a law which permits, which necessitates loopholes."

"So that an outlaw like yourself . . ."

---

* At least in the so-called higher species.

Second Dialogue

". . . can accept being put on the Index, disgraced by the human laws and customs of his time and his country; but cannot accept living outside the bounds of nature— that is a contradiction in terms. If there are bounds here, it is because we have drawn the boundary lines too soon."

"And for your own convenience, you draw these boundary lines so as to exclude, no longer to include, love. Perfect! May I be so bold as to ask if you thought this up all by yourself?"

"Others have helped me. Reading Lester Ward, for instance, inspired the notion, or at least helped to make it clear to me. Have no fear—I'll explain what I mean, and in the end I hope to show you that my theory, far from being subversive, actually confers upon or restores to love that eminent dignity which M. de Gourmont so delighted in stripping from it."

"Better still! I'm listening to you . . . But you mentioned reading . . . ?"

"Lester Ward: an American economist-biologist, a supporter of the gynecocentric theory. I'll start by explaining his ideas; with him, though unknown to him, we come to the heart of the matter."

iii

"Androcentrism, which Lester Ward counters with his gynecocentrism, is scarcely a theory at all, or if it is one, then it is a virtually unconscious theory; androcentrism is the practice, commonly adopted by naturalists, of considering the male as the representative type of each animal species, of giving it first place in descriptions of the species, and of treating the female as no more than secondary.

"Now Lester Ward starts from this point: that if need be, nature could dispense with the male."

"How kind of him."

"Bergson, whom I know you admire, has a sentence that corresponds to your remark. *Sexual generation,* he says in *Creative Evolution, is perhaps no more than a luxury for the plant.* The female is certainly indispensable. *The male element,* writes Lester Ward, *was added at a certain stage . . . with the sole purpose,* he adds sagaciously, *of assuring the crossing of hereditary strains. The creation of the male element was the first game, the first sport in nature.*"

"Anyway, whether sport or task, the male is here; where does your gynecocentrist want to relegate him?"

"I must deal with his ideas as a whole. Listen—I think this passage will enlighten you as to the meaning of his theory."

He took a sheet of paper and read from it.

"The normal color of birds is that of the young and of the female; the male's color is the result of his excessive variability. The females cannot vary in this way, they represent the center of gravity of the biological system. They are that 'stubborn power of permanence' Goethe speaks of. The female not only typifies the race but in fact, all metaphor aside, she is the race." *

* Lester Ward, *Pure Sociology,* 1911, part II, chapter XIV.

Second Dialogue

"I don't see anything very remarkable in that."

"Listen to another passage: *The change, or progress, as it may be called, has occurred exclusively in the male, the female undergoing no modification. This is why it is so often said that woman represents heredity and the male represents variation.* And here Ward quotes a sentence from W. K. Brooks: *The ovum is the material medium by which the law of heredity is manifested, while the male element is the vehicle by which new variations are added.*† Excuse the style. I'm not responsible for that."

"Keep going. As long as I'm interested in what's being said, I pay no attention to that."

"Ward claims to infer from all this the superiority of the female element. *The idea that the female sex is naturally and really the superior sex seems incredible,* he writes, *and only the most liberal and enlightened minds, possessing a widespread biological knowledge, are capable of coming to terms with it.* He can say what he likes—if I refuse to 'come to terms with it,' it's because the notion of superiority seems to me unphilosophical. It is enough for me to understand clearly this differentiation of roles, and I presume you understand it as I do."

"Go on."

"In support of his thesis, Ward undertakes a kind of history of the male element in the animal species during the various stages of their evolution. With your permission, we'll follow him for a moment. He portrays

† Ibid.

this element as something indefinite to begin with, scarcely differentiated in the hermaphroditism of the coelenterates; then as something distinct, but a tiny parasite of a female fifty or a hundred times larger than itself, clinging to her, and carried by her as a simple instrument of fertilization, just as women in certain savage societies wear a phallus hanging around their necks."

Never having heard of these monstrosities before, I showed my amazement: "How serious is this natural history? Your Ward is very farfetched—can we take his word for all this?"

Corydon stood up and walked over to his bookcase.

"These animal species and their behavior have been known for some time. Chamisso, the delicate author of *Peter Schlemihl*, was one of the first to deal with them. Here are two volumes of Darwin, dated 1854, entirely devoted to the study of cirripeds, an order of animals that for a long time was not distinguished from the molluscs; most cirripeds are hermaphrodite, but according to Darwin there exist dwarf males in some species—males that are extraordinarily simplified to the point of being no more than what is required for their function: sperm-bearers without mouth or digestive apparatus, three or four of them found on each female. Darwin calls them *complementary males*. They are also frequent among certain kinds of parasite crustaceans. Look," he said, opening an enormous book of zoology, "this shows you the hideous female of the *Chondracanthus gibbosus*, with her dwarf male attached to her . . .

Second Dialogue

"But from these scholarly works I shall retain no more than what can advance my theory: in my book expounding it, I show that the male element, after having begun by being entirely complementary, retains in itself, and tends to retain more and more, the surplus substance not utilized for the advantage of the species and modifiable according to the individual—the substance of variations."

"I don't follow—you're going too fast."

"Lester Ward will help you: *Throughout the lower orders*, he observes, *an excess in the number of males over females is the normal condition.* —Yes, but now it's my turn to point out that in these lower species in which the males predominate numerically, the male has no purpose other than procreation; he achieves this and expires without doing anything else. Bergson's *luxury* here consists in the number of individuals, since in order to fertilize a female a single male was sufficient; here we find waste, superfluity, and, in the form of individuals, substance not employed for the advantage of the species; luxury, gratuitousness. As the number of males in proportion to the number of females is reduced in the animal scale, this luxury, this gratuitousness are, so to speak, concentrated: the individual transforms them into himself. Ward's postulate remains the same: *It is essential that no female risks remaining unfertilized.* Hence, constant* overproduction of the male element— overproduction of the males and overproduction of the

---

* Or almost constant: at the end of this dialogue we shall consider certain species which, while appearing to constitute an exception to this law, in fact confirm my theory.

seminal substance. But while the female, even with a single egg, is captured by the race as soon as fertilization has been accomplished, the male remains unoccupied, endowed with a strength which he will soon enjoy."

"Doubtless he will require this strength to protect the race and to provide for the female's needs, while the interests of the race immobilize her?"

"Let me call Ward to the rescue once again. *Nothing is more false*, he writes, *than the often-repeated statement, inspired by the androcentric theory, that the so-called superior males devote this newly acquired strength to the protection and feeding of the female and the young.* Examples follow. Do you want to hear them?"

"You can lend me the book. Let's go on."

"Not too fast. We haven't quite covered the ground yet."

He put the two volumes of Darwin back on the shelf, sat down again, and continued more calmly.

"*It is essential that no female risks remaining unfertilized.* Yes, but one male is enough to fertilize one female—indeed, a single ejaculation, a single spermatozoon is sufficient to do so. Yet the male element is everywhere predominant. Either the males are numerically predominant, while the male is exhausted in procreation; or, when the proportion of males is lowered, each male becomes capable of fertilizing a greater number of females. What is this admirable mystery? Before studying its cause, I should like to show you its consequences."

Second Dialogue

"The first result, among the lower species—the fatal result is that if the female (as occurs, we have said, among the cirripeds, for example) does not allow several males to live with her simultaneously (and even then she secures only a ridiculously inadequate proportion, and mates with only one of them)—the inevitable result is that there will be a considerable number of males that will never experience . . . normal love, since coitus is denied them; a number considerably greater than the number of males who will be able to satisfy themselves 'normally.' "

"Let's get on to the species where the proportion of males decreases."

"With them the procreative power increases, and the problem, instead of confronting the mass, confronts the individual. But the problem remains the same: overabundance of procreative substance; more seed, infinitely more seed than fields to sow."

"I'm afraid you're playing right into the hands of the neo-Malthusians: the males will copulate several times with the same female; several males with one female . . ."

"But usually the female, immediately after fertilization, remains at rest."

"I see you are speaking of animals."

"With the domestic species, the solution is simple: one stallion is kept for the herd, one cock for the henhouse, and the remaining males are castrated. Nature does not castrate. Consider the useless and unpleasant fattening which the extra tissues form in castrated animals: oxen, capons are good for nothing but our tables. Castration makes the male into a sort of female: he will assume the female type, or more accurately, he will retain it. Yet whereas in the female this extra substance is immediately utilized for the race, what happens to it in the uncastrated male? It becomes material for variation. Here, I believe, is the key to what is called 'sexual dimorphism,' which in almost all the so-called superior species makes the male into a creature of show, of song, of art, of sport, or of intelligence—a creature of play.

"I've come across a remarkable passage in Bergson," he continued as he rummaged through his papers, "which seems to me to throw some light on the subject . . . Ah, here it is: he's talking about the opposition between two orders of phenomena which has been observed in living tissues, *anagenesis* on the one hand, *catagenesis* on the other. *The role of the anagenetic energies*, he says, *is to raise the inferior energies to their proper level for the assimilation of organic substances. They construct the tissues. On the other hand* . . . For catagenesis the definition is less striking, but you will already have grasped it: the female role is anagenetic, the male role is catagenetic. Castration, by making an unutilized anagenetic force triumph in the male, shows how natural the gratuitous expenditure is for him."

"Yet this surplus of elements, in the uncastrated males, can surely provide material for variation only if it is not expended externally. I mean: variation is undoubtedly in direct relation with the degree of . . . chastity."

"I don't think you should look for any moral there. The shrewdest zootechnicians limit the stallion's sexual expenditure to one emission a day; yet when the stallion exhausts himself from earliest youth in any number of irregular expenditures, he no doubt loses his vigor, but not any of the characteristics of his dimorphism.* The catagenetic force, inhibited in the castrated animal, assumes first place in the stallion."

"I was thinking of the tenors who compromise their top notes by too much lovemaking . . ."

"The most one can say is that these dimorphic characteristics attain their finest development in the so-called higher species only when seminal expenditure is reduced to its minimum. Chastity, on the other hand, is not of great advantage to the female; no catagenetic force will ever find material for variation in what she withholds from the race . . . Listen! Right next to my Bergson quotation is one from Perrier's speech at the annual session of the Five Academies, in 1905. It's nothing out of the ordinary, but . . ."

"Go on, read it."

". . . If, in the inferior animals, the eggs can gain possession of these reserves with such avidity that they destroy the creature that has produced them, one understands that they are hostile to any useless developments

---

* Such dimorphism is scarcely perceptible among equine species, but what I say about it applies just as well to all other families.

*in the superior animals, and this is why the female sex
so often retains the plumage or coat of the young, which
is only transitional for the males. Hence all this is perfectly coordinated . . ."*

"Anagenesis."

*"On the other hand, everything seems to be contrast,
contradiction, and paradox when it comes to the male
sex. Yet this sex too has its characteristic. This showy
finery, these glamorous means of seduction are in fact
no more than a vain display of dead parts, the sign of a
senseless expenditure, of an inordinate prodigality of
the organism, the mark of a temperament which exter-
nalizes but knows no economy."*

"Catagenesis—mad catagenesis! . . ."

*"The sumptuous colors of butterflies are contained in
tiny scales, elegant no doubt but utterly lifeless . . . The
coloring of birds develops in feathers which are quite
dead, etc.* I can't read you the whole speech."

"But isn't that just the way sculpture and painting—
all art, in fact—developed, on just those parts of the
Greek temples and the cathedrals which had ceased to
be useful?"

"Yes, that's the way the formation of triglyphs and
metopes is explained, for instance. One might say that
only what escapes utilitarian domination can serve aesthetic finality. But let's not take that line now—it will
only distract us . . .

"The female sex, Perrier concludes, *is therefore in
some sense the sex of physiological foresight; the male
sex, that of sumptuous but unproductive expenditure . . ."*

Second Dialogue

"Isn't this where natural selection comes in? Didn't Darwin teach us that everything like the nightingale's song and these fine colors and astonishing forms are there only to attract the female?"

"Here I go back to Ward. Please excuse so many quotations, but the theory I'm formulating is a bold one, and I need all the support for it I can find: *The female is the guardian of the hereditary qualities. Variation can be excessive . . . it requires regulation. Woman is the balancing force of nature . . .* And a little farther on: *While the voice of nature, speaking to the male in the form of an intense appetitive interest, says to him: Fertilize! it gives the female a different command and says to her: Select!* To tell you the truth, I mistrust this 'voice of nature.' Taking God out of creation and replacing Him by 'voices' isn't much of an advance . . . This eloquent nature seems to me to be the same one that 'abhors a vacuum.' That kind of scientific mysticism seems to me just as harmful to science as religion ever was. Never mind! Let's take the word 'voice' in its widest metaphorical sense—I would still deny that it says to the male *fertilize!* and to the female *select!* It simply says, to both sexes, *take pleasure!* It is the voice of the glands which demands satisfaction, of the organs which insists upon functioning—organs formed according to the requirements of their precise function but guided solely by the need for pleasure. Nothing more.

"Logically speaking, it is less difficult to accept this supposed 'selection' of the female; but in most cases it is the fittest male that wins her and which she is forced to select—by elimination."

Second Dialogue

He was silent a moment, as though at a loss; relighting the cigarette he had allowed to go out, he went on: "We have briefly examined the consequences of the over-production of the male element (and I propose to return to it in the second part of my book, which I'll tell you about tomorrow, if you like); now we'll try to ascertain its cause."

v

"I use the word 'prodigality' for any expenditure out of proportion to the result achieved. Several pages of my book will deal, in a general way, with prodigality in nature: prodigality in forms, prodigality in numbers. Today we shall deal only with the latter. The surplus number of eggs, to begin with; then the superabundance of seminal substance.

"The large white Doris (a kind of sea slug) lays approximately 600,000 eggs, according to Darwin's 'most moderate computation.' *Yet this Doris was not very common*, he writes; *although I was often searching under the stones, I saw only seven individuals.** For this prodigality in the number of eggs implies no great diffusion of the species in which it occurs; on the contrary, it often seems to imply a *difficulty in succeeding* proportionate to the prodigality expended. *But*, Darwin adds, *no fallacy is more common with naturalists than that the numbers of an individual species depend on its powers*

---

* *Voyage of the Beagle*, 1901.

48

of propagation. We may assume that with some hundred fewer eggs, the Doris species would become extinct.

"Elsewhere Darwin speaks of how the wind shakes clouds of pollen from the conifers, and of how these trees are then smothered by *these thick clouds of pollen, just so that a few grains can fall by chance on the ovules.* If one were to attribute to the pollen grain some instinct which guided it toward the ovule, then nothing would explain, nothing would excuse such profusion. But perhaps with a smaller proportion of the male element, the mysterious act of fertilization would remain too much a matter of chance.*

"Is not the explanation, the *raison d'être* of this almost constant superabundance of the male element† to be found then in a certain indecision of the sexual instinct (if I dare couple the words 'indecision' and 'instinct')? Must we not admit, sooner or later, that the imperative quality of this instinct remains somewhat

---

* At the end of this section we shall see that if, in certain species, the instinct acquires precision, then the proportion of the male element immediately decreases.

† "The males seem infinitely more numerous than the females, and probably not more than one percent of them can fulfill their destiny" [!] M. de Gourmont acknowledges in *The Physiology of Love* after relating Blanchard's story "of the naturalist who captured a female silkworm, put it in his pocket, and made his way home escorted by a cloud of more than 200 males." See Darwin's *Descent of Man* (selection in relation to sex): "The males of certain species can become so common that the point is reached when almost all remain celibate. With the small silver-blue cockchafers which frequent the plants of waterside spiraea and which are collected for mounting in jewelry (*Hoplia cerulea*), one finds only one female to every 800 males; with maybugs (*Rhizotrogus oestivus*) there is also only one female to every 300 males" (Edmond Perrier, *Le Temps,* August 1, 1912).

ambiguous? And will not nature be comparable to a marksman who, knowing his lack of skill and fearing to miss the target, compensates for the inaccuracy of his aim by the quantity of shots he fires?"

"I thought you weren't so concerned with finalities."

"You're right: the 'why' concerns me less than the 'how,' but it is often no easy matter to disentangle the two questions. Nature constitutes a network without beginning or end, and who knows where to grasp this unbroken series of links; moreover, nothing remains more problematical than knowing if each link finds its *raison d'être* in its predecessor or in its successor (if indeed it has a *raison d'être* at all), and if the whole book of nature, to be properly understood, should not be read backward—in other words, if the last page is not the explanation of the first, the final link the secret motive of the beginning . . . A man concerned with finalities would read the book from back to front."

"For pity's sake, no metaphysics!"

"You want the preceding link? Would you be satisfied if some biologist came along and told us that the overproduction of males is caused by insufficiency of nourishment—after previously proving . . . for example, that an overabundance of food tends to produce a greater proportion of females (I have no idea whether this is a duly established fact*), but that such an overabundance

---

* Perhaps the most interesting observations on this point are Fabre's on the Osmias, which according to him predetermine the sex of their eggs by the size of the site chosen for hatching the larvae. In the same way bees produce either queens, drones, or workers according

of food never occurs in the state of nature, or at least never for long; for suppose that this overabundance did exist and that according to this theory it led to an over-production of females: then, either a certain number of females would run the risk of remaining unfertilized (which is contrary to Ward's first postulate), or they would all be fertilized, in which case the overproduction of individuals in the next generation would result in a shortage of food which, in turn, would result in a greater proportion of males, so that in two generations the balance would be restored. For in principle one can assume, providing no decimating factor intervenes, that there is never *too much* food and that there is always the greatest number of mouths to be fed from nature's store. —How does that explanation strike you?"

"I don't know. Let's try the 'succeeding link.' "

"All right, let's take the chain from the other end: if I observe that the sexual instinct is inadequate—yes,

---

to the size of the cell they construct for the egg and the food they give to the larva. The male is the *minus habens*.

I have also made note of W. Kurz's observations on the cladocerans (reported by Claus): "The males generally appear in the autumn; they can also appear at any other season of the year, whenever, as has been recently shown, as a result of modifications in their environment, the biological conditions become 'unfavorable' (*Zoologie*). René Worms, in his remarkable study *La Sexualité dans les naissances françaises*, concludes that, contrary to widespread belief, the greater proportion of male births in a nation is a sign of poverty; that as wealth increases, so this proportion diminishes until finally, in a state of general prosperity, it gives way to a greater proportion of female births. "It will be seen," adds Perrier, whose same article in *Le Temps* I am quoting, "that this conclusion is in entire agreement with the one I myself have set forth."

insufficiently precise to ensure the perpetuation of the species, then the surplus of males can be considered as a necessary precaution . . ."

"Rather, let's say that any species in which the number of males remains insufficient becomes extinct."

"If you like. Coming from opposite directions, the student of finality and the evolutionist meet at the same point. The surplus of males is necessary for the perpetuation of the race *because* the sexual instinct is insufficient."

"That is the point which still has to be proved."

"In a moment we shall observe its insufficiency in nature; but first I'd like to examine with you the possible causes of this flagrant insufficiency, and steal a march on my subject. Let us proceed step by step."

"I'm following. You were saying: with a smaller proportion of the male element, the act of fertilization would remain too much a matter of chance . . ."

"It remains a bold enterprise. There are two elements here, male and female, which must be joined together, with no better inducement than pleasure. But to obtain pleasure, this joining together of the two sexes is not indispensable. Granted the male is necessary for the fertilization of the female; but the female is not indispensable for the satisfaction of the male. And this famous 'sexual instinct' may well dictate to the animal the automatism whereby pleasure will be obtained, but its counsel is so indecisive that in order to obtain procreation at the same time, nature must resort to such subtle tricks, on occasion, as those involved in the reckless fertilization of orchids."

Second Dialogue

"You're speaking as if you had finality in view once more."

"Sorry: creation exists—I don't know whether it might not, but it *does*. The only thing to do is to explain it as economically as possible. We are faced with races of creatures that perpetuate themselves by reproduction and that can reproduce only by fertilization. As I say, it is a difficult enterprise, a reckless gamble, and the chances of failure are so formidable that this surplus of males was doubtless necessary to offset the number of fiascos."

"As you see, nature's *intention* reappears."

"My metaphor has misled you. There may be a God, but there is no *intention* in nature; I mean, if there is intention, it can only be from God. There is no intention in pleasure, which is the sole inducement to that gesture which makes procreation possible; but whether pleasure succeeded the inclination or preceded it, I maintain that it has freed itself—has become self-sufficient and its own goal.* Wasn't it Chamfort who reduced love to 'the contact of two epidermises'?"

"And to 'the exchange of two fantasies.'"

---

* In the same way, not one of the male's sports, after perhaps having played its part in natural selection, has failed to free itself and become its own goal.

I shall repeat here what Fabre said about the *Locustidae*, which he might just as well have said about birds: "What is the good of this well-tuned instrument? I shall not go so far as to deny it a role in the formation of couples. But that is not its fundamental function. Above all, the insect utilizes it to express its joy in being alive, to celebrate the delights of *existence* . . ."

Second Dialogue

"Let's leave fantasy to human beings; for animals there's nothing but the pleasure of contact."

"Are you saying that that's what the sexual instinct comes down to?"

"No, but I'm saying that without the help of certain expedients which I'll mention in a moment, it's by no means certain—as you humorously suggested a moment ago—that the male will always select the female and achieve fertilization. As I have said, the enterprise is an arduous one, and nature will not bring it off without the intervention of adjuvants."

vi

Too new for my taste, this theory had disconcerted me at first, but I quickly recovered.

"You must be joking, Corydon: no sexual instinct! I'm no expert in natural history, that's for sure, and I admit I'm not particularly astute as an observer, but in the country, where I spend the autumn months hunting, I've seen dogs from the village over a kilometer away coming to spend the night at my gate, howling for my bitch . . ."

"That must make it hard to sleep."

"Luckily it only lasts a short while."

"Why is that?"

"My bitch, thank God, doesn't stay in heat for long."

I immediately regretted my remark, for Corydon's expression turned sly as soon as he heard it, and I began to feel uneasy. But I had gone too far not to answer when he continued.

"And this . . . condition lasts . . . ?"

"About a week."

"And it occurs . . . ?"

"Twice a year, maybe three times . . ."

"And except for these periods . . . ?"

"Corydon, you're making me lose my patience! What are you trying to make me say?"

"That at other times the dogs leave your bitch in peace, which you know as well as I do. That except for set periods, it is impossible to make a dog mount a bitch (which incidentally is not always so easy even at the right times)—first of all because the bitch refuses and second because the male experiences no desire to do so."*

"Well, isn't that precisely because the sexual instinct warns them that at such times there can be no fertilization?"

"What well-informed animals! And doubtless it is out of virtue that your learned dogs abstain at ordinary times?"

"Any number of animals make love only when the females are in heat."

"You mean: only the females make love . . . Because if there is a season for love, poetically speaking, there are no such periods, strictly speaking, for the males (particularly for male dogs, which we happen to be considering at the moment, and generally for all domestic animals, which are quite unconcerned with the seasons).

* "Here, *as always with animals*, mating occurs only when the females are in heat. Otherwise they will not tolerate the male's approach" (Samson, *Zootechnie* [*Lutte des ovidés*], II.

Second Dialogue

For the male, any season is good; for the female, only the periods when she is in heat. And that is the only period that the male desires her.* Wouldn't this be so because the odor which the female then gives off attracts the male to her?† Wouldn't it be this odor, and not actually your bitch, which lured the keen-scented dogs from the neighboring village and which kept them aroused even though they couldn't reach her . . . ?"

"It's a combination of the two; and since the odor wouldn't exist without the bitch . . ."

"But if, after establishing that the bitch does not excite the dog without this odor, we then establish that this odor does excite the dog, independently of the bitch, haven't we then made that kind of *experimentum crucis* Bacon would accept?"

"What preposterous experiment are you suggesting now?"

"The one that Rabelais so obscenely, which is to say so accurately, relates in the second book of his *Pantagruel* (chapter XXII). There we read how Panurge, to avenge himself for a certain lady's unkindness, secured a bitch in heat, cut her into pieces, tore out the ovaries,

---

* "The sexual instinct in the male is aroused at all times exclusively by the odor given off by the female in heat; in the female it is normally manifested only at fixed periods and under the intrinsic influence of the ovulation cycle, occurring in her own ovaries. Furthermore, when she has been fertilized, this same instinct is dormant during the entire period of her gestation and during a part of the nursing period, which in most of our domestic animals amounts to about a year" (Samson, *loc. cit.*).

† ". . . a greater activity of the vaginal glands, which secrete a product giving off a particular odor which the male's sense of smell infallibly makes him recognize" (Samson, V).

and, having ground them into mincemeat, made a kind of ointment to spread on the cruel woman's gown. Here I should let Rabelais describe what happened.

Getting up, Corydon proceeded to take the book from his shelves and read this passage:

. . . .

. . . .

. . . .

"Can you consider that as anything more than a fantasy—or anything better?"

"Which in itself would doubtless not be enough to convince us," he continued; "but nature is constantly providing us with equally conclusive examples:* this odor is so powerful and so disturbing to the animal's senses that it exceeds the role which sexuality assigns it (if I may use such an expression) and like a simple aphrodisiac intoxicates not only the male but also other females that approach the female in heat and even make clumsy attempts to mount her.† Farmers separate a cow

---

* Let us quote those reported by Fabre: one female of the small night emperor moth attracts a flock of male emperor moths into Fabre's study. These insects besiege the wire cage containing the female; she remains indifferent to them, perched on a twig Fabre has hung in the middle of the cage. If the next day Fabre shifts the female to another cage and perch, the males still flock to the first cage left at the other end of the room and cluster around the first perch in particular, for it is impregnated with subtle emanations. However apparent the female is to them (and Fabre is careful to place her in their path), they pass her by and assail the old perch, and when they have knocked it to the floor, they cluster around the place on the chair where it first landed.

† A bitch of my acquaintance lives on good terms with two cats; when the female cat is in heat, the bitch becomes very excited and sometimes tries to mount her like a tomcat.

in season from the rest of the herd when she is being molested by other cows . . .† Finally, and this is the point I want to make: if the sexual appetite is roused in the male by the female's periodic odor, *this is not the only time at which it is thus aroused.*‡

"It has been claimed, and with reason I presume, that the male can actually excite other males by bearing the odor of a recent coitus and hence the evocation of the female."

"It would be very strange if this odor, which vanishes so quickly from the female, 'immediately after fertilization,' as Samson says, should persist when transferred to another animal.* But be that as it may! I can assure you that I have seen dogs assiduously pursuing other dogs which have never engaged in coitus; and they resume the pursuit at each new encounter without any regard for the season."

"If the facts you're reporting are accurate—and I agree to accept them as such . . ."

"You can hardly do otherwise!"

† "One even sees cows in season trying to mount each other, *either because they have the notion of thereby provoking the male, or because their visual representation of the desired act compels them to attempt a simulation of it,*" M. de Gourmont writes, after saying a few lines earlier that "in general, animal aberrations require only the simplest of explanations."
He then adds: "A marvelous example, because so absurd, of the motive force of images" (*The Physiology of Love*). I am afraid it is more absurd than marvelous.
‡ "One also sees certain animals practicing the love of the males for their own sex," Montaigne remarks rather strangely in *The Apology for Raimond Sebond.*
* Even M. de Gourmont knows that "under normal conditions, the female must cease emitting her sexual odor immediately after intercourse" (*The Physiology of Love*).

Second Dialogue

"How do you explain that they have never been entered in the Great Book of Science?"

"First of all, because that 'Great Book' doesn't exist; also because there has been very little observation of the things I'm telling you; and finally because it is as difficult and as rare to observe well as to think well and to write well; a good observer is enough to make a great scientist. The great man of science is just as rare as any other man of genius; any number of half-scientists will accept a traditional theory to guide or misguide them, and to do all their 'observing' for them. For a long time everything confirmed nature's abhorrence of a vacuum; yes, all the *observations*. For a long time everything confirmed the existence of two different electricities attracted to each other by an almost sexual instinct. Even now everything confirms this theory of the *sexual instinct* . . . So that the stupefaction of certain breeders, when they discover homosexual behavior precisely in the species they raise, is really ludicrous; and each of these modest 'observers,' confining his attention to the species he is studying, discovers such behavior and believes he must regard it as a monstrous exception. 'Pigeons appear to be particularly [!] prone to sexual perversion, according to M. J. Bailly, the widely experienced breeder and *splendid observer*,'* we read in Havelock

* Such phenomena have been so frequently observed that even in Belèze's outdated *Dictionnaire de la vie pratique* we find the following under *Pigeon*: "It occasionally happens that the nest which should constitute a couple [?] consists instead of two males or two females; one perceives the presence of two females because they lay two sets of eggs; and the presence of two males because they disturb the pigeon cote." [?!]

59

Second Dialogue

Ellis; and Muccioli, 'an Italian scientist who is *an authority on pigeons* [!], states that practices of inversion are observed among certain Belgian [!] carrier pigeons, *even in the presence of many females.*' "

"So that La Fontaine's *Two Pigeons* . . . ?!"

"Never fear, they were French. Another observer reports the same habits among ducks, being a duck breeder. Lacassagne, specializing in chickens, observes them in chickens. Wasn't it among your partridges that Bouvard or Pécuchet claimed to discover them? . . . Yes, nothing is more ridiculous than these timid observations—unless it's the conclusions some people draw from them, or simply the explanations they supply for them. Doctor X, having established the great frequency of intercourse between male maybugs, argues to excuse these turpitudes . . ."

"Yes, I was just telling you: only the male that has just copulated and that is still impregnated with the odor of the female can offer a pretext for assault . . ."

"Is Doctor X quite sure of what he is saying? Was it really only after copulation that the males in their turn were mounted? Did he scrupulously *observe* this, or did he conveniently *assume* it? . . . I suggest this experiment: I'd like to know whether a dog completely deprived of its sense of smell would thereby be condemned to . . ."

"To homosexuality pure and simple?"

"Or at least to celibacy—to the complete absence of heterosexual desires . . . But just because the dog desires the bitch only when she is in good odor, so to speak, it doesn't necessarily follow that ̄his desires are dormant the rest of the time. And from this derives the great frequency of their homosexual activity."

"Let me ask you the same question in my turn: have you scrupulously *observed* this, or aren't you just conveniently *assuming* it?"

"You could easily notice such a thing for yourself, after all; but I know that usually people walking by and seeing two dogs copulating assume the sex of each dog from the position it takes.* Let me tell you a story: On one of the Paris boulevards, two dogs were stuck together in the pitiful fashion which you are familiar with, I imagine; each satisfied, they were struggling to get free; their divergent efforts were scandalizing some of the onlookers and amusing the rest; I approached. Three male dogs were prowling around the group, doubtless attracted by the smell. One of them, bolder or more excited than the others, unable to restrain himself any longer, attempted to assault the pair. I watched him perform the most incredible antics for quite a while in his attempt to mount one of the captive creatures . . . There were several of us watching the scene, as I told

* "The same oscillations of the body, the same lateral flagellations are frequently practiced between males. While the one on top wriggles and turns its legs in all directions, the one underneath remains still. Sometimes a third and even a fourth silly creature [!?] comes and climbs on top of the others. The one of the top of the pile wiggles its front legs vigorously and makes rhythmical movements with its body; the others remain motionless. This is how the rejected ones briefly delude themselves"—J. H. Fabre (*Cèrocomes*), vol. III. Has this patient observer observed whether it is really after *rejection* that these homosexual activities occur? Is it only because they have been rebuffed that these males copulate with each other? Or do they not proceed to such activities straightaway?

61

you, for one reason or another; but I guarantee I was the only one to notice that it was the male dog, and only the male dog, that the newcomer was trying to mount. He deliberately ignored the female; he struggled a little longer to obtain his ends, and since the other dog was attached and could scarcely resist, he had very nearly succeeded . . . when a policeman appeared on the scene and then and there dispersed both the actors and the spectators."

"May I suggest that the theory you are proposing—a theory doubtless prompted by your temperament—also preceded the curious observations you have recounted, and that you yourself have succumbed to the temptation you so vehemently criticize in your scientific colleagues: observing for the sake of proving?"

"First of all, it has to be admitted that it is very difficult to suppose that an *observation* can be the result of chance, and that it occurs to the mind as the fortuitous answer to a question the brain has not asked. The important thing is not to force the answer. Have I succeeded? I hope so; I cannot be absolutely certain, being as fallible as anyone else. All I ask is that the answers that nature whispers or shouts to me be verified. What I want to make clear is this: having questioned nature with a different set of preoccupations, I have received a different set of answers."*

"Couldn't nature be questioned without any preoccupations at all?"

---

* What observations could seem more unprejudiced, more honest than those of the painstaking Fabre concerning the cerceris? Observations completely invalidated or at least *reversed*, today, by Marchal.

"Precisely in this matter, it seems to me difficult. Sainte-Claire Deville, for example, says he has *observed* that goats, rams, or dogs, shut away from females, grow agitated and excited among themselves 'with a sexual excitement which no longer depends on the laws of rut and which compels them to copulate with each other.' Please notice that exquisite euphemism 'which no longer depends on the laws of rut'! Sainte-Claire Deville adds: 'It is sufficient to introduce a female to restore the entire situation to order.' Is he really sure of such a thing? Has he really observed it? He is *convinced* of it—which is not at all the same thing. My example comes from a report to the Academy of Moral Sciences on 'Boarding Schools and Their Influence on the Education of the Young.' Does he speak as a scientist, or only as a pedagogue? And what about this saving female he introduces into the kennel or stable against all the 'laws of rut'— must she always be in heat? We know that if she is not, the males will not come near her; and if instead of one female we were to introduce twenty, the males would still continue their pursuit of each other without any concern for the females."

"Perhaps Sainte-Claire Deville's observations were mistaken from the beginning?"

"What a cowardly way out. Sainte-Claire Deville's initial observation of these animals' homosexual activity was quite correct; it was from then on that his flagrant inventions began—if he had agreed to carry his investigations further, he might have discovered that the intervention of one or more individuals of the opposite sex was in no way sufficient to 'restore the entire situation to order,' except for about one week of the year, when these females could arouse desire; and that the rest of the time these homosexual activities persisted 'even in the presence of many females,' as Muccioli says."

"No doubt you would call these lascivious activities the most innocent frolics?"

"Although such activity may be highly significant, it cannot be said that these animals find, except on very rare occasions, complete satisfaction in homosexuality. How imperious then must this desire be which compels them to it all the same."

"Of course you are aware," I rashly proposed, "that the bitches too do not always participate willingly, even when they are in heat. The one I was telling you about just now was a thoroughbred; I wanted her to have a litter. With great difficulty I got hold of a perfectly matched male, but when it came time to breed her, what a business! First of all, the bitch kept pulling away; the male was wearing himself out in his clumsy efforts; then, when she seemed docile, the male was completely dispirited . . . It was only after five days that we managed to get her mounted."

"Excuse me," Corydon said, smiling, "are you telling me this as evidence against my theory?"

I could not retreat. "I'm contributing my share of impartial observations to the subject under discussion."

"For which my thanks . . . Yes; all breeders know about these difficulties; on farms, many inseminations have to be assisted, and the 'sexual instinct' appears in the guise of a farmhand."

Second Dialogue

"Then how are such things achieved in the state of nature?"

vii

"For the past hour I've been explaining to you that this is why the male element is so abundant. Your famous 'sexual instinct' makes up for what it lacks in precision by its supersaturation. On farms where only the number of stallions needed are kept, the risk would be too great if man did not occasionally lend a hand. In Samson's *Zootechnie* there are no less than nine pages devoted exclusively to the servicing of horses; for the stallion, he informs his students at Grignon, 'easily loses the way'; and 'when it has reared, the groom must take hold of its penis in order to guide it,' etc.

"But as you were saying, the difficulty does not arise only from the male's clumsiness; the female, for her part, becomes restive and tries to withdraw; often it is necessary to hold her down. Two explanations have been given for this remarkable apprehension: the first consists of ascribing to the animal sentiments of a Galatea, inflaming the male's desires by a pretended amorous flight; the second consists of ascribing to Galatea the sensations of the animal which both desires and fears..."

"Isn't it likely that these two explanations coincide...?"

"I promise you that some seem not to have noticed

it; and here again M. de Gourmont proposes the second in opposition to the first."

"You, no doubt, have a third?"

"Herewith: that the sexual instinct is as undetermined in the female as in the male . . . Yes, the female will feel *complete* only when fertilized; but if she craves fertilization as a result of a secret organic need, it is vaguely pleasure and not precisely the male which she desires; just as the male, for his part, does not desire precisely the female, and still less 'procreation,' but simply pleasure. Both of them quite plainly seek sexual pleasure.

"And that is why we so often see the female fleeing the male and at the same time offering herself for pleasure, returning to the male, who alone can provide her with it. I agree that they can find a complete and fulfilled pleasure only with each other (at least the female only with the male) and that their organs will find their perfect employment only in coitus. But it seems that *they* do not know it—or only in such a chaotic fashion that it scarcely amounts to what we would ordinarily regard as an instinct.

"Now for fertilization to occur, two indeterminate desires must be made to converge, at least once. Hence that persuasive aroma which the female will exude at propitious times, imperatively designating her presence to the male; an aroma, or no doubt a still subtler emanation, which the insect's antennae will perceive; which will be exuded not only by the female but, in certain species of fish for instance, by the eggs which are fertilized directly by the male only after they are laid by the female, who seems to be excluded from the game of love.

"It is through a single door, briefly and very narrowly ajar, that the future must insinuate itself. For such an inconceivable victory over chaos and death, nature is granted prodigality! Nor can this be regarded as 'thoughtless expenditure,' for to incur such waste is not to pay too dear for nature's victory . . ."

" 'Waste,' you said . . ."

"Yes, waste, from the point of view of utilitarian finality. But it is upon this waste that art, thought, and play will be able to grow and to flourish. And just as we saw the two forces, anagenetic and catagenetic, set in opposition to each other, in the same way we shall see two possible forms of devotion similarly contrasted: the male's for his art, his sport, his song; the female's for the race. Can you think of a finer drama than this, in which these two forms of devotion face each other in a sublime conflict?"

"Let's not encroach on tomorrow's conversation. Besides, I don't want to abandon natural history without asking you a few more questions. Do you claim that homosexual tastes are to be found in all animal species?"

"In many—perhaps not in all. I can't really say, for lack of adequate information . . . But I very much doubt whether they are to be found in those species where coitus is most difficult, or at least most complicated and requiring most effort; with dragonflies, for instance, or with certain types of spider which practice a kind of artificial insemination, or with certain others where the male, either immediately following or even during coitus, is devoured by the female . . . Here, as I say, I make no assertions; I content myself with suppositions."

"A strange supposition . . ."

"It might suffice, to establish it as a fact, to discover that in species where coitus is acrobatic or dangerous, the male element is proportionally less. For instance, these remarks of Fabre astonish me: 'In the second half of August I began to encounter the adult insect. . . . The pregnant females become more frequent every day. Their frail companions, on the other hand, are quite rare and occasionally I have great difficulty in completing my pairs.' Here he is talking about the praying mantis, in which the female always devours the male.

"This rarefaction of the male element ceases to appear paradoxical when it is compensated by the precision of the instinct. Once the male must be sacrificed by the female, it is vital that the desire which impels him to coitus be imperious and precise; *and once desire becomes precise, the excess of males becomes unnecessary*. On the other hand, it is vital that the number of males* increase once the instinct slackens; and the instinct slackens once the danger is removed from pleasure —or at least once pleasure becomes easy.

"So that this disconcerting axiom, that the number of males decreases as the difficulty of coitus increases, is really nothing but the natural corollary of what I was proposing from the start: the surplus of males (or

---

* Or the proportion of the male element—I mean: the superabundance of seminal substance, once the individual does not find in coitus the fulfillment of its life cycle.

the superabundance of the male element) compensates the imprecision of the instinct; or if you prefer: the imprecision of the instinct finds its proof in the superabundance of the male element; or to put it still another way . . ."

"I follow you, I follow you."

"I want to make my point absolutely clear: (1) The instinct becomes increasingly precise as coitus becomes more difficult. (2) The number of males is proportionately less as the instinct becomes more precise. (3) Therefore the number of males decreases as the difficulty of coitus increases (for those males sacrificed to love by the female!); no doubt if there were some other way of achieving sexual pleasure, they would immediately abandon the dangers of coitus—and the species would become extinct. But no doubt, too, nature gives them no other means of satisfaction.*

---

* It is remarkable that precisely in this species (*Mantis religiosa*) and despite the small number of males, each female is prepared to consume an inordinate number of them; she continues to offer herself for coitus and remains attractive to the male even after fertilization; Fabre tells of how he saw one female welcome and then devour seven males in succession. The sexual instinct, which we see here to be imperious and precise, immediately exceeds its purpose. I was naturally led to wonder whether, in these species where the number of males is proportionately inferior, where consequently the instinct is more precise and hence no unemployed substance remains on which the catagenetic force can operate, no "material for variation"— whether under such circumstances dimorphism does not operate in favor of the female sex—or to put it differently: whether the males of these species are not *less* showy in appearance than the females. And this is precisely what we can establish in the case of the praying mantis, the male of which is "dwarf, frail, drab, and shabby" (to borrow Fabre's adjectives) and cannot aspire to that "many-colored posture" in which the female exhibits the strange beauty of her

Second Dialogue

"Again, I am only speculating."

"I'll think over what you've said. As I come to understand you better, it grows increasingly clear that your
conclusion isn't warranted by your premises. I admit
I am indebted to you for making me reconsider these
questions, which are usually ruled by a sort of authori-
tarian principle imposing a ready-made set of convictions
which one refrains from verifying. So here is the point
I reach with you:

"Yes, the sexual instinct exists, despite what you say;
it functions, though you say otherwise, with a singular
insistence and precision; but it is compelling only at
certain times, when the two elements come into play. In
order to respond infallibly to the female's momentary
proposition, the sexual instinct confronts her with the
permanent desire of the male. The male, you were saying, is all gratuitousness; the female all foresight. The
only heterosexual relations (of animals) are for the
purpose of fertilization."

"And the male is not always satisfied with these."

"For some time now we've lost sight of your book.

---

broad, diaphanous, green-edged wings. Moreover, Fabre takes no
notice whatever of this singular reversal of attributes, which here
corroborates my theory. These considerations, which I relegate to a
footnote—since they depart from my main line of reasoning—where
I fear that they will pass unnoticed, seem to me of the greatest
interest. Having taken this new and admittedly speculative theory to
its conclusion, the joy I experienced on discovering a confirming
example coming, so to speak, to meet me, is comparable only to that
of Poe's treasure hunter who unearthed the casket full of jewels at
the exact spot where his deductions had convinced him it must be.
—Perhaps I shall someday publish further observations on this
subject.

Second Dialogue

Do you have some conclusions to draw from this first part?"

"Just this, which I would propose to those who consider finalities: if, despite the almost constant superabundance of the male element, nature requires so many expedients and adjuvants in order to ensure the perpetuation of the race, will we be surprised to learn that just as many constraints of just as many kinds are necessary in order to deter the human species from its tendency toward that behavior you have declared 'abnormal'; and that so many arguments, examples, invitations, encouragements, of so many kinds, are required in order to maintain human heterosexuality at the desired coefficient?"

"Then you will grant that there is some good in this constraint on the one side and in this encouragement on the other."

"I will grant it until tomorrow, when we shall examine the question no longer from a zoological but from a human point of view, and consider whether perhaps such repression and encouragement have not gone too far. But in return, will you for your part acknowledge that homosexual tastes no longer seem to you so contrary to nature as you claimed this morning? That is all I ask of you today."

THIRD DIALOGUE

"I've thought a lot since yesterday," I said to Corydon as I came in. "Let me ask you something: do you really believe in the theory you were developing?"

"At least I'm entirely convinced of the reality of the phenomena which prompted it. As for claiming that the explanation I offer for them is the only possible one or the best, far be it from me to be so presumptuous. But I might add that, in my opinion, this is of no great importance. I mean that the importance of a newly proposed system, of a new explanation of certain phenomena, is not to be assessed solely by its accuracy, but also and above all by the energy it affords the mind for new discoveries, new observations (even if these were to invalidate the said theory), by the paths it opens, the barriers it removes, by the weapons it provides. The main thing is that it offers what is new and at the same time opposes what is old. Today it may seem to us that the whole of Darwin's theory is tottering; but shall we deny for that reason that Darwinism advanced science more than it thwarted it? Shall we say that De Vries is right as opposed to Darwin? No—no more than Darwin or even Lamarck was right as opposed to X."

"According to you, we would no longer even dare to say that Galileo . . ."

"Let me make a distinction between the establishment of facts and the explanation one gives of them. The explanation remains undetermined; but far from always following the new observations, it frequently precedes them; sometimes, in fact often, we find theory anticipating observation, and observation only subsequently confirming the mind's bold proposition. Take my own notions as hypotheses; I shall be satisfied if only you grant them a certain initiating virtue. Once again, the facts are there, and you cannot deny them. As for the explanation I give of them, I am ready to abandon it as soon as you produce a better one for me."

i

"Yesterday we were able to consider," he continued, "the preponderant role played by the sense of smell, that signaling sense of the sexual instinct in animal intercourse. Because of the sense of smell, the male's indeterminate desire will deliberately turn toward the female—and solely toward the female in heat. One might say without too much exaggeration that the 'sexuality' of the genetic instinct (to use the modern jargon) lies in the male's olfactory sense. Strictly speaking, there is no selection of the female by the male; as soon as she goes into heat—into good odor, as we say—the male is flung upon her, led by the nose. Lester Ward, in a passage I have spared you, insists on this fact that 'all females are alike for the male animal,' and in actuality, they *are* alike, as we have seen, the male alone being capable of variation and individualization. The female, in order to attract him, has no resource except her odor; she needs no other; she does not have to be beautiful; it is sufficient that she be in good odor. Choice—if choice is not simply the victory of the fittest—choice remains the female's privilege; once she chooses according to her taste, we touch on aesthetics. Consequently it is the female, Ward further insists, who exercises the power of selection, who creates what he calls 'the male's efflorescence.' For the moment I shall not attempt to decide whether this superior beauty of the individual male in most insects, birds, fish, and mammals—a beauty which may be the result of the female's good taste—is properly to be found in the human race as well."

"I've been waiting for you to come to the point for a long time."

"Provisionally, to reward your patience, let us first notice this: the male nightingale's coloring is not much brighter than the female's, but the female doesn't sing. The male's efflorescence is not necessarily a charm, a grace; it is a luxury; and it may take the form of song, of some sport, or even of intelligence.

"But let me abide here by the order of my book, where I approach this important point only later on."

"Follow whatever order you like. I agree to your postponing as long as possible the questions you find troublesome, providing you come back to them eventually . . . For I am determined from now on not to let you drop the subject until you have poured out all your knowledge and your logic as well—until you have used up all your arguments. But tell me now how you begin the second part of your book."

"This is how: I begin by stating that the sense of smell, so crucial in animal intercourse, plays no role whatever in human sexual relations; if it does intervene, it does so on supererogatory grounds."

"Is that observation really a matter of much interest?"

"To me this difference seems so remarkable that I wonder if M. de Gourmont, by making no mention of it in his book, by not taking it into account in his identification of man with the animals, failed to notice it, or simply omitted it—or very conveniently conjured it out of sight."

"I've never yet seen him embarrassed by an objection. Perhaps it was just because he didn't attach the same importance to this difference that you do."

"An importance which will become apparent to you, I hope, in the consequences it involves, which I shall now try to explain.

"The woman, let us say, no longer has the periodic odor of the menses with which to attract the man; no doubt some other attraction replaces it; natural or artificial, this attraction remains independent of her periods, not governed by ovulation. The desired woman is desirable at all times. Let us go further and say that while the female animal attracts the male and indeed permits him to approach only during the periods when she is in heat, it is precisely during the woman's menstrual periods that man usually abstains from sexual intercourse with her. Not only are these periods devoid of sexual attraction, but they entail a kind of prohibition; it matters little to me, for the moment, whether this prohibition is physical or moral, whether we are to regard it as a momentary disgust of the flesh, a survival of ancient religious taboos, or an intellectual disapproval—the fact remains that it is at this point that man separates himself —and very distinctly so—from the animals.

"Henceforth the sexual appetite, while still remaining imperious, is no longer on such a short rein; the olfactory nerves hitherto had governed its function; now it assumes a wider scope. Love (and I am reluctant to use this word so soon, but I shall have to, sooner or later)— love immediately turns into a sport—a sport without a season, a game played without rules."

"I trust that doesn't mean that everyone is absolutely free to play it as he pleases."

"No, for desire remains no less imperious in this sport; but at least it will be more diverse; the imperative, to be as categorical, will become more individual; yes, suited to each individual. Furthermore, the individual will no longer desire the female in general, but one woman in particular.

"Spinoza tells us: *The affections of animals differ from the affections of men as much as their nature differs from the human*; and later, when he is speaking of humanity specifically: *The pleasure of one man is as naturally distinct from the pleasure of another as the nature of the one differs from the nature of the other—*

adeo gaudium unius a gaudio alterius tantum natura discrepat, quantum essentia unius ab essentia alterius differt."

"Montaigne and Pascal, and now Spinoza; you certainly know how to choose your sponsors. As you interpret it, this 'gaudium unius' tells me nothing worthwhile. 'I'm very much afraid . . .' as Pascal used to say. But go on."

He smiled briefly, then continued.

ii

"On the one hand, constant attraction; on the other, selection made no longer by the female in favor of the male, but by the man in favor of the woman . . . Does this not give us the key, or more accurately the justification, of this inexplicable preeminence of feminine charm and grace?"

"What do you mean by that?"

"I mean that from one end of the animal scale to the other we have been obliged to acknowledge, in all animal mating, the glaring supremacy of male beauty (whose purpose I have tried to explain to you); that it is quite disconcerting to see the human couple suddenly reverse this hierarchy; that the reasons hitherto provided for this sudden reversal remain either mystical or irrelevant—to the point where certain skeptics have wondered whether the woman's beauty did not reside chiefly in the man's desire and whether . . ."

I did not let him finish. I was so unprepared to hear him produce an argument based on common sense that at first I did not grasp his meaning; but as soon as I did, I was determined not to give him time to retract, and I exclaimed:

"You've helped us out of a narrow corner, for which my thanks. I now realize that this 'constant attraction' of the woman begins precisely where the other one leaves off; and no doubt it is of considerable importance that the man's desire is no longer dependent on his sense of smell but on his more artistic and less subjective sense of sight; this is surely what allows a culture and the development of the arts . . ."

Then, yielding to that confidence which the first sign of good sense had irresistibly inspired in me:

"There's a certain piquancy in owing to a uranist the first sensible argument in favor of what you call the preeminent grace and charm of the fair sex; but I admit that up to now I had been unable to find any other, except in my own feelings. So now I shall be able to reread without embarrassment certain passages in M. Perrier's speech to the Academy, which you lent me yesterday . . ."

"Which ones do you mean?"

Pulling the pamphlet out of my pocket, I read: "*Watching the flattering tints of a party gown sparkle in the sunlight or under the chandeliers of a great ballroom* (description) . . . *one might suppose that adornment has been the exclusive intention of the daughters of Eve. . . . It seems that only for their embellishment do such things exist as silver, gold* (list), *diamonds* (list), *flowers* (list), *feathers* (list), *butterfly wings . . . ; men have not yet dared approach the 'creation' of these*

*delights by which the very mind of Woman seems mo-
mentarily to beguile us—her witty, exquisite, or trium-
phant hats. . . .* (You must forgive him: he probably
saw some in his audience.) *By a very sharp contrast,
whereas women's age-old taste for adornment grows
and subsists, at least in our civilized countries, men
separate themselves increasingly from any effort . . ."*

"I told you: the male's efflorescence is not necessarily
grace and charm."

"Let me finish reading: *Even the somber dress of the
middle class seems too cumbersome: it is made lighter,
shorter, and reduced to a simple jacket, so that on the
occasions when women are present we figure as humble
grubs gliding among the flowers."*

"All very courtly."

*"This evolution is entirely characteristic; it separates
the human race from the higher animal species, quite as
much as any of its physical or psychological attributes.
It is in fact exactly the opposite of what is manifest in
much of the animal realm, where the male sex is the one
particularly favored; it is thus favored in all respects,
even in the lower forms of life, provided they are capable of a certain activity."*

"Is that the passage which embarrassed you? May I
ask why? . . . Actually I should have thought it was the
kind that would please you . . ."

"Don't play the innocent! You couldn't help noticing
that Perrier, under the pretense of praising the fair sex,
is praising only its veneer."*

* A similar naïveté appears in these lines by Addison, from *The
Spectator* (No. 265): "It is observed among birds, that nature has

Third Dialogue

"Yes; what I called just now the 'artificial attraction.' "

"The phrase strikes me as disingenuous; but I see what you had in mind. And I was thinking just now that it was anything but adroit for our scientist to belabor the issue, for after all, to tell a woman, 'You're wearing a delightful hat,' is hardly as flattering as to say, 'How lovely you are.' "

"Hence we had better say, 'How becoming to you that hat is!' But is this all that embarrasses you? I seem to recall that toward the end of his speech, Perrier drops the question of adornments and transfers his praise to the person who assumes them; hand me the speech . . . Here: *Ladies, you have triumphed with the transparency of your complexions, the crystalline purity of your voices, the soft elegance of your gestures, and those graceful lines which have inspired the caressing brush of a Bouguereau* . . . What could be prettier than that? Why didn't you read those lines?"

"Because I know you don't like Bouguereau."

"You're too kind."

"Stop teasing and tell me what you think of this."

"I admit that so much artifice, so constantly sum-

___

lavished all her ornaments upon the male, who very often appears in a most beautiful headdress: whether it be a crest, a comb, a tuft of feathers, or a natural little plume, erected like a kind of pinnacle on the very top of the head. As nature, on the contrary, has poured out her charms in the greatest abundance on the female part of our species, so they are very assiduous in bestowing upon themselves the finest garniture of art. The peacock in all his pride does not display half the colours that appear in the garment of a British Lady, when she is dressed either for a ball or a birthday. . . ."
Or should we take this as irony?

moned to nature's aid, distresses me. I recollect that passage from Montaigne: *It is not so much modesty as artistry and prudence which makes our ladies so circumspect in denying us entry to their closets before they are painted and prepared for their public appearances.* And I rather doubt if in Pierre Louÿs's fantasy *Tryphème* the habitual and frank display of the charms of the fair sex, and the custom of displaying themselves stark naked in town and country, would not produce a result contrary to the one he appears to predict; if man's desires for the opposite sex were not considerably cooled by such an enterprise. *It remains to be seen,* said Mlle Quinault, *whether all the objects which arouse in us so many lovely and naughty things because they are hidden from view, would not have left us calm and cold by a perpetual contemplation; for there are examples of such things.* —Actually there are certain tribes, and in fact the handsomest, where the fantasy of *Tryphème* is realized (or at least was realized some fifty years back, before the missionaries got to work), Tahiti for instance, when Darwin landed there in 1835. In a few eloquent pages he describes the splendor of the natives, then: *I was much disappointed in the personal appearance of the women; they are far inferior in every respect to the men. . . .* Then, after having noted their need to compensate this inferior beauty by adornment,* he goes on: *The women appear to be in greater want of some becoming costume even than the men."*

* "The custom of wearing a white or scarlet flower in the back of the head or through a small hole in each ear, is pretty" (*Voyage of the Beagle*).

Third Dialogue

"I had no idea Darwin was a uranist."

"Whoever said he was?"

"Isn't that what this passage suggests?"

"No! Are you going to make me take M. de Gourmont seriously when he writes: *It is the woman who represents beauty. Any divergent opinion will forever be regarded as a paradox or as the product of the most deplorable of sexual aberrations.*"

" 'Forever' strikes you as too much?"

"Don't get excited. As far as I know, Darwin was no more of a uranist than many other explorers who, traveling among naked tribes, have marveled at the beauty of the young men—no more of a uranist than Stevenson, for instance, who in speaking of the Polynesians acknowledges that the beauty of the young men greatly exceeds that of the women. Which is precisely why their opinion matters to me and why I agree with them, not as a puritan, but as an artist, that modesty is becoming to women and that it suits them to be veiled —'*quod decet*.' "

"Then what is the significance of what you were just saying—your argument in favor of the grace and charm of the fair sex that seemed so pertinent . . ."

"I was going to explore the possibilities of this line of reasoning: when the female made the choice and in a sense controlled natural selection, then we saw that selection working in the male's favor; reciprocally, it works in the woman's favor, since it is now the man who chooses."

"Hence the triumph of feminine charm and grace— yes, that's just what I had understood."

Third Dialogue

"So hastily that I have not been able to pursue my notion further. I was about to draw your attention to the fact that whereas among the animals the male's efflorescence can be transmitted only to the male, *women certainly transmit most of their characters, including beauty, to their offspring of both sexes* (the sentence comes from Darwin's *Descent of Man*). So that the strongest men, by taking the loveliest wives, are working for the beauty of the race, but not more for the beauty of their daughters than of their sons."

"Now it's your turn to watch what you're saying: the more you depreciate woman's beauty in favor of man's, the more you will be showing the triumph of that instinct which still makes her beauty preferable to me."

"Or the more expedient the good offices of ornament and the veil."

"Ornament is no more than a spice. As for the veil, it can entertain for a moment, provoke desire by postponing a more complete revelation . . . If you are not susceptible to feminine beauty, so much the worse for you, and you have my sympathy—but don't go trying to convince me of general aesthetic laws based on a sentiment which, despite all you can say, will remain an individual one."

iii

"And perhaps it's an 'individual sentiment' in Greek sculpture, to which we must return whenever we speak of beauty, that shows me man naked and woman veiled?

Third Dialogue

Yes, in this almost constant predilection of Greek art for the body of the boy and the young man, in this insistence on veiling the woman's body, instead of acknowledging purely aesthetic reasons, you prefer to see 'the product of the most distressing sexual aberration'?"

"Suppose I choose to see it as just that? Are you someone to teach me the extent of pederasty's ravages in Greece? Besides, wasn't the choice of these youths as models merely a way of appealing to the vicious inclination of a few debauched patrons? And isn't it open to doubt whether the sculptor was yielding to his artistic instinct or, rather, to the tastes of those he served? After all, it's impossible for us today to take into account certain necessities or conventions which constrained the artist then and determined his choice, for instance at the time of the Olympic games—conventions which no doubt also obliged Michelangelo to paint not women but naked youths on the Sistine ceiling, out of respect for the sanctity of the place, and precisely in order not to arouse our desires. After all, if like Rousseau we were to hold art in part responsible for the singular corruption of Greek morals . . ."

"Or Florentine morals. Remarkable, isn't it, how each great renaissance or artistic exuberance is always and in whatever country it occurs accompanied by a great outburst of uranism."

"By an outburst of all the passions, you'd have to say."

"And when someone decides to write a history of uranism in its relation to the plastic arts, it is not during the decadent periods that it will be observed to flourish, but quite the contrary, in the glorious and healthy epochs—precisely those epochs when art is most spontaneous and furthest from artifice. Conversely, it seems to me that not invariably but frequently the exaltation of women in the plastic arts is the index of decadence—just as we find, in the various nations where custom decreed that women's roles in the theater be taken by boys, that the decadence of dramatic art began the day these boys were replaced by women."

"You're deliberately confusing cause and effect. Decadence set in the day when the noble dramatic art determined to please the senses rather than the mind; it was then, as a means of attraction, that women took the stage, from which you will not dislodge them again. But let us return to the plastic arts. I just thought of Giorgione's splendid 'Concert Champêtre' (which I trust you won't consider as a work of decadence), which represents, as you know, gathered together in a park, two naked women and two fully clothed young musicians."

"From a plastic or at least from a literary point of view, no one would dare claim that the bodies of these women are beautiful; *too fat*, as Stevenson says; but what radiant substance! what deep, soft, harmonious luminosity! Couldn't we say that if masculine beauty triumphs in sculpture, on the other hand woman's flesh lends itself best to the play of colors? Here, I thought, in front of this picture, here is the very antithesis of ancient art: the young men dressed, the women naked; doubtless the land where this masterpiece could be created must remain quite poor in sculpture . . ."

"And in pederasty?"

Third Dialogue

"Oh! on that score, a little picture of Titian's makes me hesitate."

"Which one?"

" 'The Council of Trent,' which right in the foreground, but set to one side in shadow, shows certain groups of nobles; two here, two there, in attitudes which leave little room for doubt. And perhaps here we should interpret this as a kind of licentious reaction against what you just called 'the sanctity of the place,' but no doubt—and as certain memoirs of the period would lead us to believe—such behavior had become common enough so that no more offense was taken at it than is shown in this little painting by the halberdiers who are standing right beside these noblemen."

"I've looked at that picture twenty times without noticing anything abnormal in it."

"We only notice—this is true for each of us—what interests us. But in this painting as in the Venetian chronicles, I should say that pederasty (which in this case, moreover, seems to turn to sodomy) strikes me as anything but spontaneous—it seems bravado, vice, an exceptional amusement for the debauched and the blasé. And I can't help thinking that in a similar way, far from being popular and spontaneous, or springing vigorously from the very soil and from the people like that of Greece and of Florence, Venetian art—as Taine called it, that 'complement of the voluptuous environment'—was a pleasure of the princely, like that of the French Renaissance under François I: an art so feminized, so dearly bought from Italy . . ."

"Try to make your notion a little clearer."

Third Dialogue

iv

"Yes, I believe that the exaltation of woman is the index of an art less natural, less indigenous than the art which the great periods of uranist art offer us. As I believe—forgive my temerity—that homosexuality in either sex is more spontaneous, more naïve than heterosexuality."

"It is easy enough to proceed quickly," I said, shrugging my shoulders, "if one has no concern about being followed."

But without listening, he continued: "This is what Barrès realized so clearly when, wanting to portray in his *Bérénice* a creature very close to nature, and obeying instinct alone, he made her a lesbian, the *friend* of 'Bougie Rose.' It is only by means of *education* that he raises her to heterosexual love."

"You're attributing to Maurice Barrès hidden intentions he did not have."

"Of which perhaps he did not foresee the consequences —that's the most you can say; for in your friend's first books, you know perfectly well that the emotion itself is intentional. *Bérénice represents for me*, he says quite dogmatically, *the mysterious power and impulse of the world.* A few lines farther on, I even find a subtle intuition and definition of her anagenetic role, when he speaks of the *serenity of her function, which is to bring to life everything that befalls her*; a function he compares and contrasts with her catagenetic 'agitation of mind.' "

Barrès's book wasn't sufficiently fresh in my memory

for me to be able to argue about it; already he was going on.

"I'd be curious to know if Barrès was aware of an opinion of Goethe's on uranism, one which bears a certain resemblance to his own notions—reported by Chancellor Müller, if I'm not mistaken, in April 1830. Let me read it to you:

"Goethe entwickelte, wie diese Verirrung eigentlich daher komme, dass, nach rein aesthetischem Masstab, der Mann weit schöner, vorzüglicher, vollendeter als die Frau sei."

"Your pronunciation is so bad I can hardly understand. Translate it for me, will you please?"

"Goethe explained how this aberration actually rose from the fact that from a purely aesthetic point of view, man was far more beautiful and more perfectly constituted than woman."

"Now that has nothing to do with what you were quoting to me from Barrès," I exclaimed impatiently.

"Wait a minute; we're coming to the connection: *Such a sentiment, once aroused, readily turns into bestiality. Pederasty is as old as humanity itself, and one can therefore say that it is natural, that it resides in nature, even if it proceeds against nature. What culture has won from nature will not be surrendered or given up at any price. (Die Knabenliebe sei so alt wie die Menschheit, und man könne daher sagen, sie liege in der Natur, ob sie gleich gegen die Natur sei. Was die Kultur der Natur abgewonnen habe, werde man nich wieder fahren lassen; es um keinen Preis aufgeben.)"*

Third Dialogue

"Possibly homosexual behavior is so deeply ingrained in the German race as to appear, to certain Germans, quite natural (as the recent scandals on that side of the Rhine would lead us to suppose), but to a truly French mind, this theory of Goethe's will remain, believe me, utterly dumbfounding."

"Since you choose to bring ethnic considerations into the discussion, let me read you these few lines from Book V of Diodorus Siculus, who to the best of my knowledge is one of the first writers to give us information about the behavior of our ancestors. *Although their women are pleasing,* he says of the Celts, *they have very little to do with them, whereas they show an extraordinary passion for male intimacy. It is their custom to fling themselves down upon animal skins which cover the ground, with a bedfellow on either side.*"

"Isn't it clear that the intention here is to discredit those whom the Greeks regarded as barbarians?"

"Such behavior, at that time, was not regarded as discreditable. Aristotle, too, in his *Politics,* happens to refer to the Celts, after complaining that Lycurgus has neglected the laws pertaining to women, which leads, he says, to great abuses, *especially when the men are inclined to let themselves be dominated by women, a habitual tendency of the warlike and energetic races. However, I make an exception,* he adds, *of the Celts and of certain other nations which openly honor masculine love.*"

"If what your Greeks say is true, you must admit we've come a long way."

Third Dialogue

"Yes, we've cultivated ourselves a little—that is just what Goethe was saying."

"And so you invite me to join him in considering the pederast as retarded, as uncultivated . . ."

"Not necessarily; but in considering pederasty as a very naïve and spontaneous instinct."

"Which will doubtless provide an excuse for the fact that the inspiration for Greek and Latin bucolic poetry is so often homosexual—didn't such poetry claim to revive the naïve behavior of Arcady?"*

"Bucolic poetry began being artificial the day the poet stopped being in love with the shepherd. But no doubt we must also see in it, as in Oriental, Arabic, or Persian poetry, a consequence of the situation the woman was placed in—a situation we will have to examine; a matter of convenience . . . As for Goethe's words, what I want to emphasize is what they admit about culture, or rather, let us say, about apprenticeship in heterosexuality. It may in fact be natural for the human child, or the primitive human, to seek indiscriminate contact, caresses, and not specifically coitus; and even that some people —that many—be more disconcerted and repelled by the

* "The curious loves, of which the ancient poets' elegies are full and which so surprised us as to appear inconceivable, are therefore possible and even probable. In the translations we have made of them, we have substituted women's names for those originally there. Juventius was changed to Juventa, and Alexis to Xanthe. The beautiful boys became beautiful girls; so we recomposed the monstrous seraglio of Catullus, of Tibullus, of Martial, and of the gentle Virgil. It was a highly chivalrous occupation *which merely proved how little we had understood the genius of antiquity*" (Gautier, *Mademoiselle de Maupin*, volume II, chapter ix).

mystery of another sex, now that no allurement of scent is there any longer to guide them. (You see that I am dropping the argument of a lesser beauty, because I do not think that sexual attraction is necessarily dependent upon it.) And no doubt some people will be irresistibly attracted by one sex rather than by the other, as Aristophanes explains in Plato's *Symposium;* but even when he is exclusively attracted by the opposite sex, I maintain that the man who is completely left to his own devices will have considerable difficulty daring to make the specific gesture, and will not always know how to invent it, and will at first betray his awkwardness."

"Love has always guided the lover."

"A blind guide; and since you are already using the word 'love,' which I wanted to keep in reserve—let me add: the more deeply a man is in love, the more awkward he will be as a lover; yes, the more closely his desire is accompanied by genuine love; yes, as soon as his desire is no longer exclusively selfish, he will be afraid of hurting the being he loves. And so long as he is not taught by some example, perhaps that of animals, or by some lesson or preliminary initiation, perhaps ultimately by the beloved herself . . ."

"Nonsense! As if the lover's desire didn't find a sufficient complement in the reciprocal desire of the beloved!"

"I'm no more convinced of that than Longus was. Remember all of Daphnis' hesitations and mistakes? Doesn't this great clumsy lover need a courtesan to instruct him?"

"Aren't the hesitations and delays you mention put

there just to afford this otherwise dreary novel a little suspense and substance?"

"Not at all! Under a thin veneer of affectation, I can see in this splendid poem the profound wisdom of what Monsieur de Gourmont calls *The Physiology of Love*, and I maintain that the *History of Daphnis and Chloë*, as our early translators used to call it, is an exemplary *natural history!*"

"And where does that get you?"

"To this: that Theocritus' uninstructed shepherds labored more naïvely; that 'instinct' doesn't always or even often suffice to solve the riddle of the opposite sex: some application is necessary. A simple commentary on Goethe's words . . . Which is why, in Virgil, we see Damoetas still mourning Galatea's escape beneath the willows, while Menalchas already enjoys a pleasure without reservations beside Amyntas:

At mihi sese offert ultro, meus igni, Amyntas.

"When the lover is beside his beloved friend, as Leonardo da Vinci admirably puts it, *he is in repose.*"

"If heterosexuality involves a certain apprenticeship, you have to admit that nowadays, in town and country alike, there is no lack of apprentices more precociously enlightened than Daphnis."

"Whereas nowadays, even (or especially) in the country, homosexual activity is quite rare, and quite discredited. Yes; as we were saying the day before yesterday, everything, in our conventions and in our laws, urges one sex toward the other. What a conspiracy, whether clandestine or avowed, to convince a boy, even before desire awakens, that all pleasure is to be experienced with the woman; that away from her there is no pleasure at all. What an exaggeration—to the point of absurdity—of the attractions of the 'fair sex,' as opposed to the systematic obliteration, disfiguration, and ridiculing of the masculine. Against which, however, certain artistic peoples will rebel—peoples among whom, as we have seen, the sense of form prevails over the concern for the 'proprieties,' in the most spirited and most admired periods of history."

"I've already answered on that point."

"Yes, by agreeing with M. Perrier, if I remember correctly, in your admiration for that constant concern with adornment by which the eternal feminine seeks, at all times and in all places, to arouse man's desire, to compensate an inadequate beauty."

"Yes: what you call the 'artificial attraction.' What have you been able to prove? That ornament is becoming to women. Where does that get us? What is more disagreeable than a man who paints his face and preens."

"Once again, the youth's beauty has nothing to do with paint; we have seen it triumphing in its nakedness in Greek sculpture. But your condemnation should be willing to make some allowances for our Western customs; for you cannot be unaware of the fact that the Orientals, among others, do not always think as we do.* Merely

---

* For instance, the delightful Gérard de Nerval, about to declare his enthusiasm, as he tells us, for two "seductive charmers" whom he sees dancing in the finest café of the Mousky in Egypt—and whom he describes as "exceedingly lovely, of proud bearing, with their Arab

adorn the youth, embellish rather than concealing, or spoiling him, set off his beauty, and you can judge the result from this passage by Montesquieu:

"In Rome, women do not appear on the stage; their roles are taken by castrati dressed as women. This has a very bad effect on morality, for nothing I know of does more to inspire the Romans to 'philosopher's love.' And further on: *During my time in Rome there were, at the Capranica theater, two little castrati, Mariotti and Chiostra, dressed as women, who were the loveliest creatures I have ever seen in my life, and who would have inspired sodomite inclinations in people whose tastes are the least depraved in this regard . . . A young Englishman, believing that one of these two was a woman, fell madly in love with him and for more than a month remained the victim of this passion. Formerly, in Florence, the Grand Duke Cosimo III had come to a similar conclusion out of pure infatuation. Judge as to the effect this must have produced in Florence, which was, in this regard, the new Athens!* (*Voyages*, I). And he goes on to quote in this connection Horace's line:

Naturam expelles furca, tamen usque recurret

Drive out nature and it returns at a gallop—to which we can give any meaning we like."

"Now I know just what *you* mean—for you, 'nature'

---

eyes brightened with kohl, their full cheeks delicately tinted"—is about "to press a few gold coins on their foreheads, according to the finest traditions of the Levant"—when he realizes just in time that his lovely dancing girls are boys, who at most deserve to have "a few paras thrown to them" (*Voyage en Orient*, I).

is homosexuality; and what humanity still has the impertinence to regard as natural and normal relations, those between a man and a woman, are for you what is artificial. Come on, I dare you to admit it!"

Corydon was silent a moment, and then said: "Of course it's easy enough to reduce my ideas to absurdity; but they won't seem quite so nonsensical in my book, where I will allow them to develop naturally from premises we have already established."

I then asked him to return to this book, which we seemed to have lost sight of for too long. He continued.

v

"Yesterday I tried to show you that the commands of the 'sexual instinct' remained, among animals, much less constantly urgent and precise than people commonly choose to believe; and I attempted to disentangle, from the complex knot which these words 'sexual instinct' bunch together, what is the simple lesson of the organ itself, its requirement, what is the compromise of taste, what the obedience to external influence, to the object; I discovered that the bundle of tendencies was compact and close-knit only at the single instant when the scent from ovulation guides the male and compels him to coitus.

"Today I was observing that no scent subjugated man's sense of smell, and that woman, possessing no peremptory power of persuasion (I mean: no irresistible if momentary attraction of the female animal in heat), could no longer claim to be anything but *constantly* desirable, and skillfully applied herself to that end, with the assent, the encouragement, and the cooperation (in our Western countries, at least) of laws, conventions, etc. I noted that artifice on many occasions and dissimulation (whose noble form is modesty), that ornament and concealment come to the aid of insufficient attraction . . . Is this to say that certain men would not be irresistibly attracted to women (or to one woman in particular) when stripped of finery? No indeed! as we see in the case of others who, despite all solicitations of the fair sex, despite all injunctions, prescriptions, and dangers, remain irresistibly attracted by boys. But I do maintain that, in most cases, the appetite which awakens in the youth is not of any very specific urgency; that he experiences pleasure in whatever form it is offered, no matter by which sex, and that he owes his habits more to outside influences than to the promptings of desire; or, if you prefer, I say that it is rare for desire to make itself specific of its own accord and without the support of experience. It is rare that the data of the first experiences be dictated solely by desire, even if they were the ones that desire would have chosen. There is no vocation easier to pervert than that of the senses, and . . ."

"Well, what of it? . . . Oh, I see what you're getting at: you're already suggesting that if each boy were left to himself and if outside reprimands did not interfere—in other words, if civilization were to slacken—homosexuals would be even more numerous than they are . . . Now it's my turn to serve up Goethe's words: *What culture has won from nature will not be surrendered or given up at any price.*"

FOURTH DIALOGUE

"A book appeared recently," he said, "which has provoked a certain amount of scandal. (And I admit that I myself could not avoid feeling a shock of disapproval as I read it.) Perhaps you know it?"

Corydon then handed me the treatise *On Marriage* by Léon Blum.

"Amusing," I said, "now that it's your turn to talk about disapproval. Very amusing. Yes, I've read it. I think it's clever, and for that reason quite dangerous. The Jews are past masters in the art of disintegrating our most cherished, our most venerable institutions—the very ones that are the pillars and foundations of our Western civilization, for the sake of who knows what license and laxity of morals which are fortunately repugnant to our good sense and our Latin instinct for social values. I've always thought that this might well be the most characteristic feature of their literature—especially of their theater."

"People have protested against this book," Corydon went on, "but no one has refuted it."

"Protests are quite enough."

Fourth Dialogue

"But the problem still remains, and evading it is not the same thing as solving it—however outraged' one might be by the solution Blum advocates."

"What problem?"

"The one directly connected with what I was saying the day before yesterday: the male has much more to expend than is required in order to answer to the reproductive function of the opposite sex and to ensure the reproduction of the species. The expenditure to which nature prompts him is quite difficult to regulate and risks becoming prejudicial to law and order as Western peoples understand them."

"Hence that nostalgia for the harem in Blum's book, which as I say is repugnant to our morals and to our Western institutions, which are essentially monogamous."*

"We prefer brothels."

"Shut up!"

"Let's say: prostitution. Or adultery. There's no getting around it . . . Unless you repeat the great Malthus's arguments: *Chastity is not, as some suppose, an enforced virtue: it is based on nature and on reason; indeed this virtue is the sole legitimate means of avoiding the vices and the misery which the law of population engenders.*"

---

* It is of interest to quote Napoleon's words here: "Woman is given to man to bear him children. Yet one woman could not suffice man for this purpose; she cannot be his wife when she is suckling; she cannot be his wife when she is sick; she ceases to be his wife when she can no longer give him children; man, whom nature besets neither by age nor by any of these disadvantages, ought therefore to have several wives" (*Mémorial*, June 1816).

Fourth Dialogue

"Of course chastity is a virtue."

"On which the laws do well not to count too much, don't you think? —In my book, I'd prefer not to have recourse to virtue except as a last resort. Léon Blum, who makes no appeal to virtue but seeks the readiest social expedient, rails at the state of affairs where prostitution, with the law's connivance, debases the members of the oldest profession. I believe that we can sympathize with him there."

"Leaving out of account the danger to public health, as soon as this prostitution escapes the revolting supervision of the state."

"That is why Blum proposes directing toward young women—and I mean the most respectable young women, the ones who will soon be wives and mothers—the anxiety and excess of our male appetites."

"Yes, I remember how that struck me as particularly monstrous and made me doubt whether Blum had ever moved in real French society, or only among Levantines."

"I can certainly imagine more than one Catholic who would hesitate to marry a girl whose previous apprenticeship had been administered by a Jew. But if you protest in the same way against each solution offered . . ."

"All right, tell me yours. Already I tremble at what I guess it's going to be."

"I didn't invent it. It's the same one ancient Greece advocated."

"Of course, there we are again!"

"Please listen to me as calmly as you can. I can't help hoping that people with the same education and background might still be able to understand each other more or less, despite all basic differences of temperament. From your earliest childhood you have been brought up as I have; you have been taught to venerate Greece, of which we are the heirs. In our schools and in our museums, Greek works occupy the places of honor; we are asked to acknowledge them for what they are: human miracles of harmony, of equilibrium, of wisdom, and of serenity; they are held up to us as examples. Furthermore, we are taught that the work of art is never an accidental phenomenon, and that we must seek its explanation, its motivation in the people themselves, and in the artist who produces it—the artist who merely gives form to the harmony which he initially realized within himself."

"We know all that. Go on."

"We also know that it was not only in the plastic arts that Greece excelled, and that this same perfection, this felicity, this aptitude for harmony is also to be found in all the other manifestations of its life. A Sophocles, a Pindar, an Aristophanes, a Socrates, a Miltiades, a Themistocles, or a Plato is no less admirable a representative of Greece than a Lysippus or a Phidias. That equilibrium which we admire in each artist, in each work, belongs to Greece in its entirety—a beautiful plant without blemish; the full development of no one branch has harmed the development of any other."

"All this has been granted long ago, and has nothing to do with . . ."

"What! Do you refuse to understand that there exists a direct relation between the flower and the plant which bears it, between the essential quality of its sap and its behavior and its economy? Are you trying to convince me that this people, capable of offering the world such mirrors of wisdom, of graceful power and of happiness, did not know how to conduct its own affairs—did not know first of all how to apply this happy wisdom, this harmony to its very life and the ordering of its morals! Yet as soon as Greek morals are mentioned, they are deplored, and since they cannot be ignored, they are turned from in horror;* we do not understand, or we pretend not to understand; we refuse to admit that they form an integral part of the whole, that they are indispensable to the functioning of the social organism, and that without them the fine flower we admire would be quite different, or would not be at all.†

"If, leaving aside general considerations, we examine one particular case, for instance that of Epaminondas— whom Cicero regards as the greatest man Greece produced—'and one cannot deny,' writes one of his biographers (Walckenaer), 'that he offers one of the most perfect examples of the great leader, the patriot and the sage'—then this same biographer finds it necessary to add: 'Unfortunately it seems all too certain that Epaminondas was addicted to that infamous taste to which the Greeks, and especially the Boeotians and the Lacedae-

---

* Not always. It is fair to cite here Herder's discerning appreciation in his *Ideas on the Philosophy of History*.

† So that one is tempted to say with Nietzsche (concerning war and slavery): "No one can escape these conclusions, if he has honestly sought the causes of that perfection attained by Greek art, and by Greek art alone" (quoted by Halévy).

monians (*i.e.*, the bravest among them), did not attach any shame' (*Biographie universelle*)."†

"Yet you must grant that such conduct occupies only an insignificant place in Greek literature."

"In what has come down to us, perhaps. And even there!‡ Don't forget that Plutarch and Plato, in speaking of love, refer to homosexual love as much as to the other kind. Then I urge you to consider (and if the observation has already been made, I don't believe much importance has been attached to it) that virtually all the ancient manuscripts by means of which we know Greece have passed through the hands of the Churchmen. The history of ancient manuscripts would be very interesting to study. We might discover if perhaps the learned monks who transcribed the texts for us did not occasionally suppress what scandalized them, out of respect for the good cause; or if at least they didn't prefer to

---

† Cf. the passages from Pascal, from Montaigne—and the accounts of the death of Epaminondas.

‡ "The *Iliad*, therefore, has for its whole subject the passion of Achilles . . . which displayed itself first as anger against Agamemnon and afterward as love for the lost Patroclus. The truth of this was perceived by one of the greatest poets and profoundest critics of the modern world, Dante. When Dante, in the *Inferno*, wished to describe Achilles, he wrote, with characteristic brevity:

> *Achille*
> *Che per amore al fine combatteo.*
> *Achilles,/who at the last was brought to fight by love*

In this pregnant sentence Dante sounded the whole depth of the *Iliad*. The wrath of Achilles against Agamemnon, which prevented him at first from fighting; the love of Achilles, passing the love of women, for Patroclus, which induced him to forego his anger and to fight at last—these are the two poles on which the *Iliad* turns" (J. A. Symonds, *Studies of the Greek Poets*, 1879, volume I).

rescue what scandalized them least. Think of the number of plays by Aeschylus, by Sophocles; out of ninety plays by the one, out of a hundred and twenty by the other, we know of scarcely seven. But we know that Aeschylus' *Myrmidons*, for instance, dealt with Achilles' love for Patroclus, and in a manner which the few verses of it quoted by Plutarch suffice to make clear to us. But let us go on. I am quite willing to believe that homosexual love occupied no greater place in Greek tragedy than in Marlowe's theater, for example (which would already be conclusive). What would that prove, if not that drama is elsewhere? Or, to express myself more clearly: that the substance of tragedy is not to be found in these happy forms of love.* On the other hand, lyric poetry is full of it, as are mythological narratives, and all the biographies, all the treatises—even though almost all of them have passed through the same expurgational sieve."

"I don't know how to answer you here—I'm not well enough informed."

"Anyway, this isn't what matters most to me. For after all, what is a Hylas, a Bathylus, or a Ganymede, compared with the splendid figures of Andromache, of Iphigenia, of Alcestis, of Antigone which we are given in the tragedies? Well! I contend that as for these pure images of womanhood, we owe them as well to pederasty. Nor do I think I am going too far when I say that the same is true of Shakespeare."

"If that's not a paradox, then I'd like to know . . ."

---

* "Happy are those who love, when they are loved in return," says Bion in his eighth idyll. Then he gives three examples of happy loves: Theseus and Pirithoüs, Orestes and Pylades, Achilles and Patroclus.

Fourth Dialogue

"Oh, you'll understand me soon enough if you merely consider the fact that, given our morals, no literature has devoted so much attention to adultery as the French; not to mention all the semi-virgins and all the semi-prostitutes. This outlet the Greeks proposed, which outrages you and which seemed so natural to them, you want to suppress. Then make your saints; or else man's desire will corrupt the wife, defile the daughter . . . The Greek girl was raised not so much with a view to love as to maternity. Man's desire, as we have seen, was directed elsewhere; for nothing seemed more necessary to the state, nor to deserve more respect, than the tranquil peace of the gynaeceum."

"So that, according to you, it was to save the woman that the child was sacrificed!"

"Perhaps you will allow me to examine, in a moment, whether any sacrifice was involved. But before I do, I should like to answer a specious objection that particularly concerns me.

"Pierre Louÿs reproaches Sparta for not having been able to produce any artists; he finds this an occasion to protest against too austere a virtue which, he says, could educate only warriors; and even these allowed themselves to be defeated. *The glory and grandeur of Sparta amount to very little for anyone who is not a blind admirer of antiquity*, writes M. de Laboulaye in a note on Montesquieu: *Did anything emerge from this military monastery but ruin and destruction? What does civilization owe to these barbarians?*"*

* *Esprit des Lois*, IV, chapter 6.

"Yes, I remember the reproach; others have made it before him."

"But I don't know how deserved it is."

"Yet the facts are there."

"First of all, don't forget that it is to Sparta we owe the Doric order, the one used at Paestum and in the Parthenon. And remember that if Homer had been born in Sparta, and born blind, he would have been cast into a dungeon. I suppose that's where you'd have to look for the Lacedaemonian artists—in the dungeons; Sparta may not have been capable of producing them, but since its only concern and pleasure was the consideration of physical perfection—and since some bodily infirmity is frequently the price of genius . . ."

"Yes, I see what you mean: Sparta systematically destroyed all its children who like Victor Hugo were born *cold, colorless, and still.*"

"Which, on the other hand, permitted it to develop the most perfect physical specimens. Sparta invented natural selection. It didn't produce sculptors, that's true, but it created the model for the pure sculptor."

"To hear you tell it, it would seem that all the models for Athens came from Lacedaemonia, the way the models for Rome come from Saraginesco today. That's absolute nonsense. You will nonetheless permit me to believe that the best specimens of manhood in Greece were not necessarily brutes, or that, reciprocally, all its artists were not bowlegged or knock-kneed. Remember that the young Sophocles at Salamis . . ."

Corydon smiled and showed with a gesture that he granted me this point. Then he resumed:

Fourth Dialogue

"One more remark on the subject of the Spartans: you're aware that in Lacedaemonia pederasty was not only admitted but even, one might say, approved. You are also aware that the Spartans were an eminently warlike people. *The Spartans*, we read in Plutarch, *were the best artisans and the most skillful preceptors in everything which concerns the art of warfare.* Further, you're aware that the Thebans . . ."

"Just a minute!" I exclaimed, interrupting him; "today I've brought my own texts." And I took out of my pocket a notebook where I had copied, the night before, this passage from *The Spirit of the Laws* (IV, chapter 8), which I then read: *We blush to read in Plutarch how the Thebans, in order to refine the habits of their young men, established by law that kind of love which should be proscribed in all nations of the world.*"

"Yes, that's just what I was telling you," he replied quite unabashed. "There's no one, today, who doesn't condemn it, and I know that it's folly to try, as an isolated individual, to be wise;* but since you insist, let's read together the whole passage from Plutarch which so outraged Montesquieu."

He fetched an enormous tome from his shelves, opened it to the *Life of Pelopidas*, and read aloud: *"In all the battles fought by the Lacedaemonians, either against the Greeks or against the barbarians, no one ever remem-*

---

* "He that opposes his own judgment against the current of the times ought to be backed with unanswerable truth, and he that has truth on his side is a fool as well as a coward, if he is afraid to own it, because of the multitude of other men's opinions. It is hard for a man to say, all the world is mistaken, but himself. But if it be so, who can help it?"—Daniel Defoe

*bered their being defeated by an enemy inferior in num-
bers or even equal in numbers* (as had just occurred at
Tegyra, in the battle which Plutarch is describing) . . .
*This battle was the first to teach all the peoples of Greece
that brave and warlike men could be bred, not only on
the banks of the Eurotas, but wherever young men
shunned disgrace, proved their courage by valiant deeds,
and preferred death to dishonor; here too men were
found to be formidable opponents for their enemies."*

"Well—I didn't make him say *wherever young men
shunned disgrace and preferred death to dishonor.*"

"I'm afraid you've misunderstood," Corydon answered soberly, "and that the inference to be drawn from
this passage is that, on the contrary, homosexuality was
never censured. Everything that follows bears this out."
He continued reading: *"The sacred band of Thebans was
organized, it is said, by Gorgidas, and was composed of
three hundred chosen men. The state provided for the
expenses of their training and maintenance. . . . There
are some who claim that this battalion was composed of
lovers, and they quote in this connection the witty words
of Pammenis: 'The lovers must be ranged close to one
another, for to break and scatter a battalion formed of
men who loved one another would be impossible; because
those who composed it would face all dangers, some
through attachment to the persons they loved and others
through fear of disgracing themselves in the eyes of their
lovers.'* That shows you," Corydon said, "what the notion
of dishonor meant to them. *There is nothing astonishing
in this,* the wise Plutarch continues, *if it be true that men
are more afraid of those who love them, even when ab-*

sent, than they are of all others, when present. Now tell me if that isn't admirable?"

"Obviously," I retorted; "but that is true even without the intervention of immoral relationships . . ."

"*Thus one of these warriors,*" he continued reading, "*struck down by the foe and seeing himself on the point of death, implores his enemy to plunge the sword through his breast: 'so that at least my lover,' he said, 'shall not suffer the shame, on finding my body, of seeing I was struck from behind.'* It is also related that Iolaus, loved by Hercules, shared his labors and fought at his side. (But no doubt you prefer to imagine Hercules with Omphale or Deianira?) Aristotle writes that, even in his day, pairs of lovers would go to Iolaus' tomb to make their vows. —So it is likely that this troop was named the 'sacred battalion' for the same reason that prompted Plato to define a lover as a friend in whom one feels something divine. *The sacred battalion of Thebes remained invincible until the battle of Chaeronea. After this battle, Philip, visiting the field of carnage, stopped at the place where the three hundred lay. It was a tangled heap of bodies and weapons, and each man had his breast pierced with a sword thrust. He contemplated this spectacle with surprise, and on learning that this was the battalion of lovers, he wept for them and exclaimed: 'Let those perish miserably who dare suggest these men were capable of committing or enduring anything dishonorable.'* "

"No matter how you try," I exclaimed, "you will never succeed in making me regard those heroes as debauchees!"

Fourth Dialogue

"But who's trying to present them as any such thing? And why won't you admit that this kind of love, like the other, is capable of abnegation, of sacrifice, even on occasion of chastity?* Nonetheless, the remainder of Plutarch's account shows us that although this love sometimes or even often led to chastity, such was not, however, its presumption. In support of this, you know that I could quote many examples from the texts, and not only from Plutarch—together, they would constitute an entire book. Would you like them? I'll keep them here at your disposal.

"I can think of no opinion more false, and yet more widely held, than that which considers homosexual conduct and pederasty as the pathetic lot of effeminate races,

* "Besides these public causes [of unhappiness], Agesilaus had a private one, his excessive love for Megabates, the son of Spithridates, which touched him to the heart, though he endeavored to master it, and especially in the boy's presence to suppress all appearance of it; so much so that when Megabates came once to receive a kiss from him, he declined it. At which when the boy blushed and drew back, and afterward saluted him at a more reserved distance, Agesilaus, soon repenting his coldness, and changing his mind, pretended to wonder why he did not salute him with the same familiarity as formerly. His friends about him answered, 'You are at fault, who would not accept the boy's kiss, but turned away in alarm; he would come to you again, if you would have the courage to let him do so.' Upon this Agesilaus paused a while, and at length answered, 'You need not encourage him to do it; I think I had rather be master of myself in that refusal than see all things that are now before my eyes turned into gold.' Thus he demeaned himself to Megabates when present, but he had so great a passion for him in his absence, that it may be questioned whether, if the boy had returned again, all the courage he had would have sustained him in such another refusal" (Plutarch's *Life of Agesilaus*, from the 'Dryden' translation, corrected and revised by Clough).

of decadent peoples, and even sees it as an importation from Asia.* On the contrary, it was from Asia that the slack Ionic order came to supplant the masculine Doric architecture; the decadence of Athens began when the Greeks stopped frequenting the gymnasiums; and we now know what should be understood by that. Uranism yields to heterosexuality. This is the moment when we see heterosexuality triumph in the works of Euripides,† along with its natural complement, misogyny."

"Why 'misogyny' all of a sudden?"

"What would you expect? It is a fact, and a very important fact—the converse of what I was pointing out to you just now."

"What was that?"

"That we owe to uranism our respect for women, and consequently the splendid figures of women and girls that we find in the plays of Sophocles and in those of Shakespeare. And just as respect for woman usually accompanies uranism, so we see the woman less honored as soon as she is more generally desired. You must see that this is a quite natural development.

"And you must also recognize that the uranian periods, if I may use such an expression, are in no way periods of decadence; I do not believe it is going too far to say, on the contrary, that the periods of great artistic flowering—the Greeks in the age of Pericles, the Romans in the age of Augustus, the British in the age of Shake-

* "The Persians, schooled by the Greeks, have learned to sleep with boys" (Herodotus, I).

† Atheneus, XIII: "Sophocles loved boys as much as Euripides women."

speare, the Italians in the time of the Renaissance, the French in the Renaissance and then under Louis XIII, the Persians in the century of Hafiz, etc.—have been the very times when pederasty asserted itself most ostensibly and, I was going to say, most officially. I would almost go so far as to say that only the periods or regions without uranism are also the periods or regions without art."

"Don't you think this might be an illusion, and that these periods seem to you especially 'uranian,' as you say, simply because their peculiar brilliance invites us to concern ourselves with them more closely, and because the works to which they owe their fame reveal more clearly and more indiscreetly the passions which animate them?"

"At last you are granting me what I was saying to you at the beginning: that uranism is quite a universal phenomenon. Well, I see that your ideas have made some progress," said Corydon, with a smile. "Moreover, I have never claimed that there was a uranian recrudescence in these celebrated periods, but only avowal and affirmation. Perhaps, however," he added after a moment, "we must believe in a certain recrudescence in times of war. Yes, I think that the periods of martial exaltation are essentially uranian periods, just as we see the belligerent peoples particularly inclined to homosexuality."

He hesitated a moment or two, then asked abruptly: "Have you never wondered why the Napoleonic Code contains no law aimed at repressing pederasty?"

"Perhaps," I replied, disconcerted, "it's because

Fourth Dialogue

Napoleon attached no importance to it, or because he reckoned that our instinctive repugnance would be sufficient."

"Perhaps it was also because such laws would have embarrassed some of his best generals. Reprehensible or not, such habits are so far from being enervating, are so close to being military, that I must admit to you I've trembled for us during those sensational trials in Germany, which even the Kaiser's vigilance could not succeed in suppressing; and even earlier, at the time of Krupp's suicide. Some people in France were naïve enough to see such episodes as signs of decadence! while I was thinking to myself: Beware of a people whose very debauchery is warlike and who keep their women for the exclusive purpose of providing fine children."

"Allow me to suggest that, faced as we are with a disturbing decrease in the French birth rate, this is scarcely the moment to incline men's desires (supposing that you could) in the direction you advocate. Your thesis is, to say the least, inopportune. Repopulation . . ."

"Don't tell me you really believe that all these inducements to love will result in the birth of a great many children? Do you imagine that all these women who offer themselves to love will consent to getting themselves knocked up into the bargain? You're joking! I tell you, the shameless stimulation of our popular imagery, theaters, music halls, and a host of publications serves only to lure woman away from her duties; to make her into a perpetual mistress, who no longer consents to maternity. I tell you that this is quite as dangerous for the state as the very excess of the other kind of debauchery—and that this other kind of debauchery necessarily involves less waste and fewer excesses."

"Don't you think you're letting your special interests and your special tastes carry you away?"

"What if I am! The important thing is not to know whether I have special interests in defending this cause, but whether it is worth defending."

"So that not content with tolerating uranism, you claim to make it into a form of civil virtue."

"Don't put foolish words into my mouth. Whether lust is homo- or heterosexual, virtue consists in mastering it. I'll come back to this in a moment. But without going so far as to claim with Lycurgus (at least according to Plutarch) that a citizen cannot be honest and useful to the state unless he has a friend,* I do claim that uranism in and of itself is in no way harmful to law and order—quite the contrary."

"But will you deny that homosexuality is often accompanied by certain intellectual defects, as is claimed by more than one of your colleagues (I'm speaking to you in your role as a doctor)?"

"If you please, we'll leave the inverts aside for now. The trouble is that ill-informed people confuse them with normal homosexuals. And you understand, I hope, what I mean by 'inverts.' After all, heterosexuality too in-

* "Their lovers too had a share in the young boy's honor or disgrace. . . . They all [the lovers] conspired to render the object of their affection as accomplished as possible" (Plutarch's *Life of Lycurgus*, 'Dryden' translation, revised by Clough).

cludes certain degenerates, people who are sick and obsessed. Alas, I must admit that all too often among the others . . ."

"Among those you have the nerve to call normal pederasts."

"Yes . . . one can sometimes notice certain character defects, for which I hold the state of our morality entirely responsible. For the same thing always happens whenever a natural instinct is systematically thwarted. Yes, the state of our morality tends to make a homosexual inclination an academy of hypocrisy, cunning, and disrespect for law."*

"Why not just say 'of crime'?"

"Obviously, if you make the thing itself a crime. But that is just what I hold against our morality; as I hold public censure of unmarried mothers responsible for three-quarters of all abortions."

* How justice can be flouted by the way in which public opinion lets itself be influenced is clearly shown by this article in *Le Matin* (August 7, 1909), which appeared after the Renard case: " *'Moral of a Trial'* . . . No defendant, for many years, has had so great an element of doubt in his favor as Renard, when he appeared before the Seine Court of Assizes. However, the jury did not hesitate, and sentenced him to hard labor. Before the Versailles Court of Assizes, the element of doubt had increased still further; yet the Versailles jury also condemned him without mercy. Before the Court of Appeal, there was a serious likelihood of the appeal being allowed; yet it was instantly rejected. And public opinion—with the few rare exceptions that one might expect [?]—always sided with the juries and the magistrates . . . Why? Because it was proved that Renard, *even granted that he was not guilty of murder*, was an odious and disgusting monster. Because there was, among the public, this impression that Renard, *though innocent of M. Remi's murder*, could not be separated from that group of individuals which society rejects from its midst and sends to stagnate in Guiana," etc.

Fourth Dialogue

"I grant you that, more generally, our morality can be held partly responsible for the lowering of the birth rate."

"You know Balzac's name for such morality?—'the hypocrisy of nations.' It is really staggering to see to what degree, in matters so serious, so urgent, so vital to the country, people prefer the word to the thing, appearance to reality, and readily sacrifice the supply of goods to the window dressing . . ."

"What are you getting at now?"

"Oh, I'm not thinking of pederasty now, but of the depopulation of France. But this would take us too far astray . . . To return to our subject, you simply must face the fact that in society, among those around you and whom you see most frequently, any number of people for whom you have the greatest respect are as much pederasts as Epaminondas or myself. Don't expect me to name them. They all have the best reasons in the world for concealing the truth. And if we should suspect one of them, then we prefer to pretend not to notice— we collaborate in this hypocritical game. The very excess of disapproval which you profess for the thing serves to protect the offender, as always happens in the case of excessive sanctions, of which Montesquieu wrote: *The cruelty of the laws prevents their enactment. When the penalty is disproportionate, we are often compelled to prefer impunity.*"

"Then what are you complaining about?"

"About hypocrisy. About lies. About misrepresentation. About that smuggler's behavior to which you drive the uranist."

Fourth Dialogue

"Then you'd like to go back to the old Greek ways?"

"If it pleased the gods! . . . and for the good of the state."

"Christianity, thank God, has risen above such a thing, sweeping away, cleansing, sweetening, and sublimating all that; strengthening the family, consecrating marriage, and, beyond that, advocating chastity; I'd like to hear what you have to say to that."

"Either you haven't listened to what I was saying, or you would have realized that my notions assert nothing contrary to marriage or damaging to chastity. I can repeat Malthus's words: *I would be distressed to say anything at all, directly or indirectly, which might be interpreted in a sense contrary to virtue.* I am not setting uranism in opposition to chastity—I am setting one form of desire, whether satisfied or not, in opposition to another. And I maintain, precisely, that the peace of the household, the honor of the woman, the respectability of the family, the health of husband and wife were more effectively preserved by Greek morality than by ours; and for the same reasons, chastity and virtue more nobly taught, more naturally attained. Do you suppose it was harder for St. Augustine to aspire to God because he had first given his heart to a friend, whom he loved as much as he ever loved a woman? Do you really suppose that their uranian education made the children of antiquity more prone to debauchery than their heterosexual education makes our schoolchildren today? I believe that a friend, even in the fullest Greek sense of the word, is of better counsel to an adolescent boy than a mistress. I believe that the education in the art of love which a Madame de Warens, for instance, could give the young Rousseau was more damaging to him than any Spartan or Theban education would have been. Yes, I believe that Rousseau would have grown up less corrupted and, as regards women, more . . . manly, if he had followed a little more closely the example of those heroes of Plutarch whom he nonetheless admired so much.

"Again, I'm not comparing chastity with debauchery of any kind, but one kind of impurity with another; and I doubt whether the young man could arrive at marriage in a more damaged state than certain young heterosexuals of today.

"I'm saying that if the young man falls in love with a young woman and if this love is authentic, then there is every chance that this love is a chaste one, not immediately crossed by desires. This is just what Victor Hugo understood so clearly when in *Les Misérables* he convinces us that Marius would rather have sought out a prostitute than even in his thoughts have raised the hem of Cosette's skirt; and Fielding in his splendid *Tom Jones*, who makes his hero tumble the whores of the inn all the more ardently for being in love with his Sophia; and this is what Merteuil plays on so cunningly in Laclos's incomparable book, when young Dancenis falls in love with the little Volange girl. But I add that, with regard to marriage, it would have been better, and less dangerous, for each of these young men if their temporary pleasures had been of another kind.

"Finally, if I may contrast one form of love with another, I am saying that the passionate attachment of

Fourth Dialogue

an older man, or of a friend of the same age, is just as often capable of self-denial as any feminine attachment. There are many examples of this, and illustrious ones.*

But here, like Bazalgette in his translation of Whitman, you deliberately replace the word 'love,' which both the authentic text and reality propose, by the non-compromising word 'friendship.'† I am saying that this love, if it is authentic, tends toward chastity‡—but only, it goes without saying, if it reabsorbs physical desire within itself, which mere friendship can never do—and that for the child it can be the best incentive to courage, to exertion, to virtue.§

"I am also saying that an older man can understand an adolescent boy's troubles better than a woman can, even one expert in the art of love; indeed, I know certain children excessively addicted to solitary pleasures, for whom I consider this kind of attachment would be the surest remedy.

"I have seen someone desire to be a girl, and a beautiful girl, from the age of thirteen till the age of twenty-

---

* See, in particular, Fielding's *Amelia*, III, chapters 3 and 4.

† "Does any more delicate and noble sentiment exist than the friendship, at once passionate and shy, of one boy for another? The one who loves dares not express his affection by a caress, a look, a word. His is a clear-sighted tenderness which is pained by the slightest defect in his beloved; it is made up of admiration, selflessness, pride, humility, and serene joy" (Jacobsen, *Nils Lyhne*).

‡ "Lubricity and the ardor of the loins have nothing in common, or indeed very little, with Love" (Louise Labé, *Débat de folie et d'amour, Discours III*).

§ Plutarch observes, in his *Life of Lycurgus*: "There goes a story that one lover was fined by the magistrates, because the lad whom he loved cried out effeminately as he was fighting."

Fourth Dialogue

two—and after that age, to become a man, says La
Bruyère (*Des Femmes*, #3)—setting rather late, in my
opinion, the moment when the adolescent's heterosexual
direction becomes explicit. Until then, his desire is indeterminate and remains at the mercy of examples, sug-
gestions, and promptings from outside. He loves at
random; he knows nothing of the love which, until the
age of about eighteen, he invites rather than is able to
offer.

"So long as he remains this *molliter juvenis*, as Pliny
calls him, more desirable and desired than desiring, if
some older man should fall in love with him, I believe,
as was believed long ago in that civilization of which
you consent to admire only the shell—I believe that
nothing can be better for him than a lover of his own
sex. I believe that such a lover will jealously watch over
him, protect him, and himself exalted, purified by this
love, will guide him toward those radiant heights which
are not to be reached without love. I believe that if,
quite the contrary, this youth should fall into a woman's
hands, this can be disastrous for him; unfortunately, we
have only too many examples of such a thing. But since,
at this excessively tender age, the youth cannot yet be
anything but the most indifferent lover, it is fortunately
not natural that a woman should immediately fall in love
with him.

"From thirteen to twenty-two (to take the age suggested by La Bruyère) is for the Greeks the age of
loving friendship, of shared exaltation, of the noblest
emulation. Only after that does the boy, according to

Fourth Dialogue

their expectations, 'desire to become a man,' which is to say, turns his thoughts to women—which is to say: to marry."

I had let him hold forth to his heart's content and had been careful not to interrupt him. When he had finished, he waited a while for some sign of opposition on my part. But without adding a word except for a farewell, I took my hat and left, convinced that to certain assertions a sincere silence is a better answer than anything one might find to say.

APPENDIX

An Open Letter to François Porché,
author of *The Love That Dare Not Speak Its Name*

January 1928

My dear François Porché,

It is said you have written a courageous book. I say so too, and that your great courage has been, while taking a position against evil, to refuse to join the chorus of barking critics; to understand—and to make others understand—that there is, in the subject you discuss, more than material for jokes, jeers, and abuse.

Your whole book reveals, in dealing with the question, not only an unusual intelligence, but also an honesty, a sense of decency, and a courtesy (particularly with regard to me) to which I am scarcely accustomed and, therefore, anything but indifferent. Furthermore, I could not read without deep emotion the page in which you recall certain wartime memories, and I want you to know the echo that the expression of your esteem and your sympathy finds in my heart.

How great was my surprise, as I went on reading, to

Appendix

encounter on page after page almost nothing I did not approve. Everywhere one feels the sincerest effort not to condemn without judgment, not to judge without understanding, and I believe it would be impossible to explore more deeply what one nonetheless disapproves.

If some objections irresistibly spring to mind with regard to what concerns my person or my writings, is this solely because my *amour-propre* is concerned? I don't think so. It seems to me that in the portrait you draw of me certain features are a little overstated, others a little distorted (though without any malevolent intention), and that, in order to give yourself more reasons to oppose my ideas, you sometimes exaggerate them a little. Finally, that development, that trajectory you detect in my work and in my character, and which the very titles of your final chapters betray—that increasing outspokenness is an invention of your own.

In this way you single out my *Immoralist*, but make no mention of the assuredly far more topical *Saul*, also published in 1902 but written five years earlier. Whether or not the play was produced did not depend on me; I did what I could to get it put on; Antoine with great courage nearly succeeded in enabling me to do so . . . I do not recall this in order to boast of having anticipated Proust, but because it is not in my nature to play the part of the Moron in the farce, who comes down from his tree to fight the bear only when someone else has already laid it low.

In the same way, according to you, I "only belatedly made the decision to write my memoirs." Several mutual friends will be able to assure you that this decision, with

Appendix

all its consequences, was made even before 1900; and not only the decision to write them, but also to publish them in my lifetime. And the same is true of *Corydon*.

This too is not very important, but it brings us back to less personal considerations: you make me more erudite than I am. In general, I have consulted life more than books, and I confess that I have never read a number of those you mention.* But after finishing yours, I reopened the *Divine Comedy* and was somewhat surprised that in your chapter on "The Tradition of Anathema," in which you mention Boccaccio, Machiavelli, and Aretino, you have not consulted Dante, the great poet of retribution.

Forbear! to these, courtesy is due, he makes Virgil say, speaking of the kind of people you are concerned with—that is, if you agree with the generally accepted interpretation. For Dante is not specific on this point, and allows the reader to make his own suppositions as to the sin committed by those he presents in Canto XVI of the *Inferno*—a sin we can deduce only by chance evidence and by knowing from other sources the lives of the damned, as for instance that Jacopo Rusticucci, according to a note of Lammenais, was married to "a shrewish wife whom he left and cast himself into infamous debaucheries." Furthermore, the preceding Canto seems to have dealt already with the same class of sinners; and this is perhaps why Dante remains so chastely unspecific.

* On the other hand, speaking of Balzac, you seem to be unaware of his extraordinary *Vautrin*, the play whose performances were abruptly halted by the censor (?) in 1840. Balzac here presents a Jacques Collin more unmasked, more revealing than in *Père Goriot* or *Lost Illusions*.

Appendix

D'un medesmo peccato al mondo lerci, he contents himself with saying (*by one same crime on earth defiled*)—speaking of that troop to which his master Brunetto Latini belongs; that troop concerning which "Ser Brunetto" will tell him: "In brief, know that all were clerks, and great scholars, and of great renown," when Dante asks him to point out *"li suoi compagni piu noti e piu somni."*

Madame Espinasse-Mongenet, in her excellent translation of the *Inferno*, also believes that both Cantos XV and XVI refer to "those who did violence to nature." But in looking for what distinguishes the next troop from the one to which Brunetto Latini belongs, the translator hesitates and doubts whether this is the nature of the sin committed. "It may well be," she adds, "that the souls are grouped according to the profession they followed in this world: on one hand, the scholars and men of letters (the sodomites with which Canto XV is concerned); on the other, the warriors and statesmen (the sodomites of Canto XVI)." And indeed, in this latter troop, come the three damned souls who hurry toward Dante: Guido Guerra, who "in his lifetime did much with counsel and with sword"—and who, Madame Espinasse adds in a note, "was a proud and valiant soldier, and a wise councillor"; then "Tegghiajo Aldobrandi, whose words of advice should have been heard and obeyed in the world above"—and who was, Madame Espinasse remarks, "a valiant knight, a man charming and wise, accomplished in the practice of arms and worthy of trust"; then Jacopo Rusticucci, whom Madame Espinasse describes as a "valiant soldier, a wealthy and good Florentine, a man of great political and moral sagacity."

Such are the homosexuals whom Dante presents us with.

And even if one refuses to recognize the damned souls of Cantos XV and XVI as the kind of sinners with whom we are concerned, being unwilling to admit that Dante could have granted them so fine a role, then one must acknowledge that Dante does not cast Sodom into hell, reserving it for Canto XXVI of the *Purgatorio*. Here there is no further room for doubt; Dante twice specifies the sin of those to whom his first words are: "O souls, certain of having, whenever it may be, a state of peace."* And once again, these sinful souls are those of poets of great renown in Dante's day.

The importance Dante attaches to these people, judging only from the attention he grants them, the *cortesia* (to borrow his own word) with which he considers it fitting to speak of them, and the extraordinary indulgence he shows on their behalf, may be partly accounted for by his feeling that Virgil himself, *"tu duca, tu signor, e tu maestro,"* after leaving him, would rejoin this troop.† Unless one prefers to say that this indulgence proceeds directly from Virgil. Surely it also derives from

* Thus these souls repented before their death, as did all those whom Dante represents in the *Purgatorio*.

† This canto deals with two troops whom Dante mingles and then separates: those who go crying "Sodom and Gomorrah!" and those who cry: "Pasiphaë enters the wooden cow, that the young bull may hasten to her lust," and who, when Dante questions them, answer rather mysteriously and inappropriately: *Nostro peccato fu ermafrodito*; to which Lammenais adds in a note: "This word here indicates the bestial union of man with animals."

the consideration both of them necessarily had for the worthy men who constituted the troop.

If I say all this, it is because your book does not. But what seems to me to be lacking above all is a chapter which your preface appeared to promise—a chapter which would constitute the answer to that question which no one seems to ask, though it seems to me an unavoidable one: What, in your opinion, is the duty, with regard to literature, of these "great men of letters"—I mean, of those who belong to this troop? Surely they are not all obliged to speak of love; but if they do, which is natural enough for poets or storytellers, must they pretend to be ignorant of the love "*that dare not speak its name*," when so often it is virtually the only love they know? For after all, to exclaim with this or that person, "Enough of such things—that's the last straw!" is all very well, but it is thereby admitting that one prefers camouflage. Do they see nothing but advantage in the disguise they implicitly recommend? For myself, I am afraid that this constant sacrifice to convention, assented to by more than one poet or novelist, sometimes among the most celebrated, rather distorts psychology and greatly misleads public opinion.

"But what about contagion!" you will say, "what about the example! . . ."

In order to share your fears, I should have to be somewhat more convinced than I am:

1. that these tastes can be so readily acquired;

2. that the behavior they involve is necessarily prejudicial to the individual, to society, to the state.

I believe that nothing is less established.

Appendix

Trendiness and fashion annoy me as much as they do you; and perhaps, on these points, more than they do you. But I believe that you are exaggerating their importance, just as you exaggerate the importance of the influence I might have.

"Whom will M. Gide convince that one should prefer green carnations to roses?" Jérôme and Jean Tharaud demanded recently. (And we know what must be understood by these two symbolic flowers.) Whom indeed? No one at all. And I cannot answer better than by asking this same question of those who accuse me of corrupting others.

If I concern myself with your book in this way, my dear Porché, it is because for the first time I find myself facing an honest adversary; I mean one not blinded by preconceived indignation. And even against the charge you make of showing off, which is perhaps directed to some extent at me, I protest only weakly. But you will grant me that it is very difficult, where dissimulation has been *de rigueur* for so long, to be frank without seeming cynical, and natural with simplicity.

Yours sincerely,
André Gide